A gift for:

_____

From:

_____

**The LORD is faithful to all his promises
and loving toward all he has made.**

Psalm 145:13

ZONDERVAN

Promises for Life for Women
Copyright © 2006 by Zondervan

Requests for information should be addressed to:
Zondervan, Grand Rapids, Michigan 49530

ISBN 978-0-310-61557-6

Excerpts taken from: *The New Women's Devotional Bible, New International Version*, copyright © 2006 by Zondervan.

Interior Design: Mark Veldheer

Printed in China
12 13 14 15 16 /CTC/ 14 13 12 11 10 9 8 7 6 5 4 3 2 1

promises
FOR life
for *Women*

ZONDERVAN®

new international version

contents

Aging

Listen to me, O house of Jacob,
    all you who remain of the house of Israel,
you whom I have upheld since you were
        conceived,
    and have carried since your birth.
Even to your old age and gray hairs
    I am he, I am he who will sustain you.
I have made you and I will carry you;
    I will sustain you and I will rescue you.

Isaiah 46:3–4

Since my youth, O God, you have taught me,
    and to this day I declare your marvelous
        deeds.
Even when I am old and gray,
    do not forsake me, O God,
till I declare your power to the next generation,
    your might to all who are to come.

Psalm 71:17–18

Charm is deceptive, and beauty is fleeting,
    but a woman who fears the LORD is to
        be praised.

Proverbs 31:30

Your beauty should not come from outward adornment, such as braided hair and the wearing of gold jewelry and fine clothes. Instead, it should be that of your inner self, the unfading beauty of a gentle and quiet spirit, which is of great worth in God's sight. For this is the way the holy women of the past who put their hope in God used to make themselves beautiful.

1 Peter 3:3 – 5

Gray hair is a crown of splendor;
    it is attained by a righteous life.

Proverbs 16:31

The righteous will flourish like a palm tree,
    they will grow like a cedar of Lebanon;
planted in the house of the LORD,
    they will flourish in the courts of our God.
They will still bear fruit in old age,
    they will stay fresh and green.

Psalm 92:12 – 14

Aging

Teach us to number our days aright,
   that we may gain a heart of wisdom.
Satisfy us in the morning with your
         unfailing love,
   that we may sing for joy and be glad all
         our days.

Psalm 90:12, 14

Do not be wise in your own eyes;
   fear the LORD and shun evil.
This will bring health to your body
   and nourishment to your bones.

Proverbs 3:7–8

"Age should speak;
   advanced years should teach wisdom."
But it is the spirit in a man,
   the breath of the Almighty, that gives him
         understanding.

Job 32:7–8

The glory of young men is their strength,
   gray hair the splendor of the old.

Proverbs 20:29

aging well

God doesn't pretend that growing older isn't tough. He acknowledges that our days are as fleeting as the grass growing in the field. We all realize that our outward beauty might fade away. Thankfully, our heavenly Father is attracted to the inner beauty that will never perish, an eternal beauty that comes from a heart radiating with God's love.

Aging is hard. For most of us, getting older means losing our youthful beauty and experiencing the breakdown of our bodies. But God tells us that there is a loveliness that comes with maturity. When we know Jesus as our Savior, we are more aware that each day brings us closer to that place where there will be no more tears, no more sorrow, no more death. Growing older for the child of God does not mean feeling useless and ugly. It means growing up and maturing into a person who looks like God, exhibiting his character qualities of compassion, abounding love and mercy. The truth is, you're getting older every day. Embrace aging as your pathway to be ever growing, ever green with an eternal purpose.

Attitude

Your attitude should be the same as that of
Christ Jesus:
Who, being in very nature God,
    did not consider equality with God
        something to be grasped,
but made himself nothing,
    taking the very nature of a servant,
    being made in human likeness.
And being found in appearance as a man,
    he humbled himself
    and became obedient to death—even
        death on a cross!

Philippians 2:5–8

*Whoever claims to live in [God] must walk as
Jesus did.*

1 John 2:6

*Do not conform any longer to the pattern of
this world, but be transformed by the renewing
of your mind. Then you will be able to test and
approve what God's will is—his good, pleasing
and perfect will.*

Romans 12:2

You were taught, with regard to your former way of life, to put off your old self, which is being corrupted by its deceitful desires; to be made new in the attitude of your minds; and to put on the new self, created to be like God in true righteousness and holiness.

Ephesians 4:22–24

Whatever is true, whatever is noble, whatever is right, whatever is pure, whatever is lovely, whatever is admirable—if anything is excellent or praiseworthy—think about such things.

Philippians 4:8

Since Christ suffered in his body, arm yourselves also with the same attitude, because he who has suffered in his body is done with sin. As a result, he does not live the rest of his earthly life for evil human desires, but rather for the will of God.

1 Peter 4:1–2

Attitude

Godliness with contentment is great gain. For we brought nothing into the world, and we can take nothing out of it. But if we have food and clothing, we will be content with that.

I have learned to be content whatever the circumstances. I know what it is to be in need, and I know what it is to have plenty. I have learned the secret of being content in any and every situation, whether well fed or hungry, whether living in plenty or in want. I can do everything through him who gives me strength.

Philippians 4:11–13

The cheerful heart has a continual feast.

Proverbs 15:15

Rejoice in the Lord always. I will say it again: Rejoice! Let your gentleness be evident to all. The Lord is near.

Philippians 4:4–5

Set your minds on things above, not on earthly things.

Colossians 3:2

a positive attitude

Our attitudes often seal our reputations. We may be honest, hard-working and smart. But if every word coming out of our mouths is whining or complaining, others begin to avoid us. The presence of a constant complainer can be off-putting. In contrast, a woman known for speaking words of encouragement and possessing an attitude of gentle contentment is inviting, drawing people to her, even if she faces times of crisis and pain. A spirit of contentment and gratitude brings peace.

Paul wrote the book of Philippians during his time in prison. Yet despite his circumstances, the book brims with joy, peace and calm. Paul knew that Christ could meet his every need, and he relaxed and even rejoiced in God's loving care. Paul encourages us to focus on things that are beautiful, pure and positive. Meditating on such things develops our ability to notice and appreciate small beauties and increases a sense of thanksgiving to God. When your gentleness is known to all, they'll realize the Lord is near and they, too, will rejoice.

Availability

Then I heard the voice of the Lord saying,
"Whom shall I send? And who will go for us?"
And I said, "Here am I. Send me!"

Isaiah 6:8

In everything that [Hezekiah] undertook in the
service of God's temple and in obedience to the law
and the commands, he sought his God and worked
wholeheartedly. And so he prospered.

2 Chronicles 31:21

Samuel went and lay down in his place. The LORD
came and stood there, calling as at the other times,
"Samuel! Samuel!" Then Samuel said, "Speak, for
your servant is listening."

1 Samuel 3:9–10

Create in me a pure heart, O God,
    and renew a steadfast spirit within me.
Do not cast me from your presence
    or take your Holy Spirit from me.
Restore to me the joy of your salvation
    and grant me a willing spirit, to sustain me.

Psalm 51:10–12

God is not unjust; he will not forget your work and the love you have shown him as you have helped his people and continue to help them. We want each of you to show this same diligence to the very end, in order to make your hope sure.

Hebrews 6:10–11

Humble yourselves, therefore, under God's mighty hand, that he may lift you up in due time.

1 Peter 5:6

The Sovereign Lord has given me an
        instructed tongue,
  to know the word that sustains the weary.
He wakens me morning by morning,
    wakens my ear to listen like one being
        taught.
The Sovereign Lord has opened my ears,
    and I have not been rebellious;
  I have not drawn back.

Isaiah 50:4–5

Availability

Now finish the work, so that your eager willingness to do it may be matched by your completion of it, according to your means. For if the willingness is there, the gift is acceptable according to what one has, not according to what he does not have.

2 Corinthians 8:11–12

Remind the people to be subject to rulers and authorities, to be obedient, to be ready to do whatever is good.

Titus 3:1

As Jesus walked beside the Sea of Galilee, he saw Simon and his brother Andrew casting a net into the lake, for they were fishermen. "Come, follow me," Jesus said, "and I will make you fishers of men." At once they left their nets and followed him.

Mark 1:16–18

You also must be ready, because the Son of Man will come at an hour when you do not expect him. Who then is the faithful and wise servant, whom the master has put in charge of the servants in his household to give them their food at the proper time? It will be good for that servant whose master finds him doing so when he returns. I tell you the truth, he will put him in charge of all his possessions.

Matthew 24:44–47

The angel said to her, "Do not be afraid, Mary, you have found favor with God. You will be with child and give birth to a son, and you are to give him the name Jesus."

"I am the Lord's servant," Mary answered. "May it be to me as you have said."

Luke 1:30–31, 38

Availability

Live a life worthy of the calling you have received.

Ephesians 4:1

Be shepherds of God's flock that is under your care, serving as overseers—not because you must, but because you are willing, as God wants you to be; not greedy for money, but eager to serve; not lording it over those entrusted to you, but being examples to the flock.

1 Peter 5:2

availability check

An ordinary day. Ordinary sheep. An ordinary shepherd. An extraordinary God with an extraordinary plan!

Moses was tending sheep—minding his own business—when he went to see a strange sight. A bush was burning without being consumed. Then God called his name from within the fiery bush. Moses immediately answered. This response indicates availability. But then God told him what he wanted.

Moses felt woefully inadequate for the task. He recited a long string of objections. Like Moses, we feel inadequate for the job: "I'm just a student, housewife or businesswoman. I'm not equipped for a rescue mission!" Fear may seize us. However, when God calls us to do something bigger than we are, he will equip us by working *through* us. We learn to rely on his strength, not on our own abilities. Simply put, God doesn't look for abilities, he looks for *avail*abilities.

Busyness

There remains, then, a Sabbath-rest for the people of God; for anyone who enters God's rest also rests from his own work, just as God did from his. Let us, therefore, make every effort to enter that rest.

Hebrews 4:9–11

It is not good to have zeal without knowledge,
    nor to be hasty and miss the way.

Proverbs 19:2

The plans of the diligent lead to profit
    as surely as haste leads to poverty.

Proverbs 21:5

Do not set your heart on what you will eat or drink; do not worry about it. For the pagan world runs after all such things, and your Father knows that you need them. But seek his kingdom, and these things will be given to you as well.

Luke 12:29–31

*Do you not know that in a race
all the runners run, but only
one gets the prize? Run in
such a way as to get the prize.
Everyone who competes in the
games goes into strict training.
They do it to get a crown that
will not last; but we do it to
get a crown that will last forever.*

1 Corinthians 9:24–25

Lord, you establish peace for us;
    all that we have accomplished you have
      done for us.

Isaiah 26:12

This is what the Sovereign Lord, the Holy
One of Israel, says:
"In repentance and rest is your salvation,
    in quietness and trust is your strength."

Isaiah 30:15

Busyness

Be still before the L ORD and wait patiently
     for him....
    Do not fret—it leads only to evil.

       Psalm 37:7–8

Man is a mere phantom as he goes to and fro:
    He bustles about, but only in vain;
    he heaps up wealth, not knowing who will
       get it.
But now, Lord, what do I look for?
    My hope is in you.

       Psalm 39:6–7

Be still, and know that I am God;
    I will be exalted among the nations,
    I will be exalted in the earth.

       Psalm 46:10

the problem of busyness

B usyness is not new or unique to our culture. It's a timeless problem. But its solution is just as timeless—to release some responsibilities to others.

Moses was a *really* busy man—he was trying to be all things to all of Israel. But it was too much for him to handle by himself. Fortunately, he had a wise father-in-law who made a great suggestion: you can't do it alone—better to delegate.

That's good advice for us, too! We simply can't be everywhere at once. Trying to be all things to all people puts us on the fast track to burnout. But when we delegate, our burden is lifted and we can focus on the things God has given us to do. Delegating also creates the opportunity for another capable person to grow into a new role. Failing to delegate may be impeding another person's God-given potential. Sometimes the best thing we can do—for ourselves and others—is to step aside so someone else can step up.

Caring for Others

The King will say, ... "Come, you who are blessed by my Father; take your inheritance.... For I was hungry and you gave me something to eat, I was thirsty and you gave me something to drink, I was a stranger and you invited me in, I needed clothes and you clothed me, I was sick and you looked after me, I was in prison and you came to visit me."

Matthew 25:34–36

Share with God's people who are in need. Practice hospitality.

Romans 12:13

Jesus said, "Whoever welcomes one of these little children in my name welcomes me; and whoever welcomes me does not welcome me but the one who sent me."

Mark 9:37

This is what the LORD Almighty says: "Administer true justice; show mercy and compassion to one another."

Zechariah 7:9–10

Jesus said, "Whoever wants to become great among you must be your servant, and whoever wants to be first must be slave of all. For even the Son of Man did not come to be served, but to serve, and to give his life as a ransom for many."

Mark 10:43–45

Defend the cause of the weak and fatherless; maintain the rights of the poor and oppressed.

Psalm 82:3

Jesus said, "When you give a banquet, invite the poor, the crippled, the lame, the blind, and you will be blessed. Although they cannot repay you, you will be repaid at the resurrection of the righteous."

Luke 14:13–14

Caring for Others

He who is kind to the poor lends to the LORD,
and he will reward him for what he
has done.

The entire law is summed up in a single command:
"Love your neighbor as yourself."

Galatians 5:14

Jesus said: "A man was going down from
Jerusalem to Jericho, when he fell into the hands
of robbers. They stripped him of his clothes, beat
him and went away, leaving him half dead. But
a Samaritan, as he traveled, came where the
man was; and when he saw him, he took pity on
him. He went to him and bandaged his wounds,
pouring on oil and wine. Then he put the man on
his own donkey, took him to an inn and took care
of him."

Luke 10:30, 33–34

Give to the one who asks you, and do not turn
away from the one who wants to borrow from you.

Matthew 5:42

caring for the poor

Often we feel overwhelmed by our own family's needs. Who has time, energy and resources to take on anything else? But we can't ignore God's command to take care of the poor—just because they seem difficult or make us feel uncomfortable. With prayer, open hearts and a little creativity, we can reach out in Christ's name. To help a homeless person, carry some gift certificates or extra sandwiches to give away if you don't want to give money. Clean out your closet and offer a warm coat or blanket. Simply treating a homeless person like a human being—and not a nuisance—might be the best witness of God's love.

There are countless ways to help meet the needs of the less fortunate. When you're obedient to the Holy Spirit's leading, you'll be amazed at how he fills you with joy.

Change

If anyone is in Christ, he is a new creation; the old has gone, the new has come!

2 Corinthians 5:17

Jesus said, "I tell you the truth, unless you change and become like little children, you will never enter the kingdom of heaven. Therefore, whoever humbles himself like this child is the greatest in the kingdom of heaven."

Matthew 18:3 – 4

Create in me a pure heart, O God,
   and renew a steadfast spirit within me.

Psalm 51:10

Listen, I tell you a mystery. We will not all sleep, but we will all be changed — in a flash, in the twinkling of an eye, at the last trumpet. For the trumpet will sound, the dead will be raised imperishable, and we will be changed.

1 Corinthians 15:51 – 52

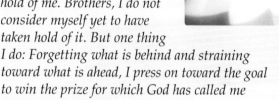

Not that I have already obtained all this, or have already been made perfect, but I press on to take hold of that for which Christ Jesus took hold of me. Brothers, I do not consider myself yet to have taken hold of it. But one thing I do: Forgetting what is behind and straining toward what is ahead, I press on toward the goal to win the prize for which God has called me heavenward in Christ Jesus.

Philippians 3:12–14

My soul finds rest in God alone;
     my salvation comes from him.
He alone is my rock and my salvation;
     he is my fortress, I will never be shaken.

Psalm 62:1–2

Change

In the beginning, O Lord, you laid the
     foundations of the earth,
and the heavens are the work of
     your hands.
They will perish, but you remain;
     they will all wear out like a garment.
You will roll them up like a robe;
     like a garment they will be changed.
But you remain the same,
     and your years will never end.

Hebrews 1:10–12

*By dying to what once bound us, we have been
released from the law so that we serve in the new
way of the Spirit, and not in the old way of the
written code.*

Romans 7:6

*Do not conform any longer to the pattern of
this world, but be transformed by the renewing
of your mind. Then you will be able to test and
approve what God's will is—his good, pleasing
and perfect will.*

Romans 12:2

letting go

L etting go of the familiar is tough. Changing careers or colleges or moving to a new city can take an emotional toll on us. It's even more difficult to leave behind old habits, attitudes and behaviors.

It is difficult to leave the familiar behind, even when God himself is saying, "It's time to move on."

We all struggle with the difficulties of letting go of the old in order to grasp the new. Take heart. God understands that letting go of the familiar is hard. Yet he has called us to move on to new life in Jesus Christ by letting go of our old worldly lives, our old habits, our old dreams—to boldly move forward without looking back. When you feel God's call to move, allow him to guide you. He will give you the grace to do whatever he has asked.

Choices

I have chosen the way of truth;
    I have set my heart on your laws.
I hold fast to your statutes, O Lord;
    do not let me be put to shame.
I run in the path of your commands,
    for you have set my heart free.

Psalm 119:30–32

Choose for yourselves this day whom you will serve,... But as for me and my household, we will serve the Lord.

Joshua 24:15

Choose my instruction instead of silver,
    knowledge rather than choice gold,
for wisdom is more precious than rubies,
    and nothing you desire can compare
      with her.

Proverbs 8:10–11

Now choose life, so that you and your children may live and that you may love the Lord your God, listen to his voice, and hold fast to him. For the Lord is your life.

Deuteronomy 30:19–20

choose wisely

God offers every single person the opportunity to "choose for yourselves this day whom you will serve." Some of us allow money to become our god, but all of our idols give us some form of pleasure, or we wouldn't idolize them. We cling to them. We don't want to let them out of our sight. We hold onto idols that take the shape of control, pride or gossip.

Sometimes, idols come in the form of people dear to us. Sometimes they're possessions. Sometimes they're much more personal, like our physique. But anything that takes our hearts and minds off the Lord Jesus becomes a tool in Satan's toolbox. And he wields these tools against us, whispering in our ears to make choices that take us further and further from God.

Our Lord is a jealous God. He wants to be the only God in our lives. Are you serving the one true God? Or are you allowing other gods to come before him?

Comfort

For this is what the LORD says:
"As a mother comforts her child,
   so will I comfort you."

On my bed I remember you, [O God;]
   I think of you through the watches of
      the night.
Because you are my help,
   I sing in the shadow of your wings.
My soul clings to you;
   your right hand upholds me.

Psalm 63:6–8

Come near to God and he will come near to you.

James 4:8

Blessed are those who mourn,
   for they will be comforted.

Matthew 5:4

*The LORD said: "I will never leave you nor
forsake you."*

Joshua 1:5

Praise be to the God and Father of our Lord Jesus Christ, the Father of compassion and the God of all comfort, who comforts us in all our troubles, so that we can comfort those in any trouble with the comfort we ourselves have received from God.

2 Corinthians 1:3–4

[God] is not far from each one of us.

Acts 17:27

Cast your cares on the LORD
 and he will sustain you;
 he will never let the righteous fall.

Psalm 55:22

[The LORD] tends his flock like a shepherd:
 He gathers the lambs in his arms
and carries them close to his heart;
 he gently leads those that have young.

Isaiah 40:11

Comfort

Jesus said, "Now is your time of grief, but I will
see you again and you will rejoice, and no one
will take away your joy."

John 16:22

Give me a sign of your goodness,
    that my enemies may see it and be put
        to shame,
    for you, O Lord, have helped me and
        comforted me.

Psalm 86:17

I will praise you, O Lord.
    Although you were angry with me,
your anger has turned away
    and you have comforted me.

Isaiah 12:1

Remember your word to your servant,
    for you have given me hope.
My comfort in my suffering is this:
    Your promise preserves my life.

Psalm 119:49–50

Jesus said, "Do not let your hearts be troubled. Trust in God; trust also in me."

John 14:1

Weeping may remain for a night,
   but rejoicing comes in the morning.

Psalm 30:5

We are hard pressed on every side, but not crushed; perplexed, but not in despair; persecuted, but not abandoned; struck down, but not destroyed.

2 Corinthians 4:8–9

   Who, O God, is like you?
Though you have made me see troubles,
         many and bitter,
   you will restore my life again;
from the depths of the earth
   you will again bring me up.
You will increase my honor
   and comfort me once again.

Psalm 71:19–21

Comfort

God, who comforts the downcast, comforted us.

2 Corinthians 7:6

The Lord bless you
 and keep you;
the Lord make his face shine upon you
 and be gracious to you;
the Lord turn his face toward you
 and give you peace.

Numbers 6:24–26

The Lord is close to the brokenhearted
 and saves those who are crushed in spirit.

Psalm 34:18

*[Jesus said,] "Come to me, all you who are weary
and burdened, and I will give you rest."*

Matthew 11:28

*Be strong and courageous. Do not be terrified; do
not be discouraged, for the Lord your God will be
with you wherever you go.*

Joshua 1:9

the need for comfort

Humans crave comfort. From infancy we cry for our mother's arms. When we are hurt, we long for tenderness.

While Israel was exiled to Babylon because of their rebellion, compassion seemed far from reach. However, even in the midst of their pain, God promised a lavish solace. "Comfort, comfort my people," he says. It's one thing to comfort someone who has been unjustly wronged. We want to nurse their wounds and soothe their pain. But what if that person hurts us? It's entirely different to welcome him or her into our arms. However, Isaiah 40 portrays that picture. The one who is right is comforting the one who is wrong. God comforts those who have wronged him. Even though we've hurt him, his merciful nature can't stand our pain.

Pause a moment. Have you turned to the Lord to receive comfort from him? The God of comfort has more than compensated for your debt.

Companionship

Above all, love each other deeply, because love covers over a multitude of sins.

Two are better than one,
    because they have a good return for
        their work:
If one falls down,
    his friend can help him up.
But pity the man who falls
    and has no one to help him up!
Also, if two lie down together, they will
        keep warm.
    But how can one keep warm alone?
Though one may be overpowered,
    two can defend themselves.
A cord of three strands is not quickly broken.

Ecclesiastes 4:9–12

Do everything in love.

1 Corinthians 16:14

If you have any encouragement from being united with Christ, if any comfort from his love, if any fellowship with the Spirit, if any tenderness and compassion, then make my joy complete by being like-minded, having the same love, being one in spirit and purpose.

Philippians 2:1–2

Be completely humble and gentle; be patient, bearing with one another in love. Make every effort to keep the unity of the Spirit through the bond of peace.

Ephesians 4:2–3

Let love and faithfulness never leave you;
    bind them around your neck,
      write them on the tablet of your heart.
Then you will win favor and a good name
    in the sight of God and man.

Proverbs 3:3–4

Companionship

A friend loves at all times.

Proverbs 17:17

My purpose is that they may be encouraged in heart and united in love, so that they may have the full riches of complete understanding, in order that they may know the mystery of God, namely, Christ, in whom are hidden all the treasures of wisdom and knowledge.

Colossians 2:2–3

This is the message you heard from the beginning: We should love one another.

1 John 3:11

Finally, all of you, live in harmony with one another; be sympathetic, love as brothers, be compassionate and humble.

1 Peter 3:8

the perfect companion

God knew that the man needed a female companion. So God caused Adam to fall into a deep sleep so that God could make a companion for him. Eve was made from Adam. The two of them shared a bond that allowed their relationship to be meaningful and intimate.

If you are married, you may not feel that God gave you the perfect match. Maybe you're disappointed or disillusioned with the man you thought was the right one for you. God can take your bitterness and transform your life into one of peace and acceptance. If you are unmarried, perhaps you fall asleep dreaming of Mr. Right but wake to find yourself still waiting. Know that God wants to be your husband and companion. Single or married, God will be with you, watching over you. You can sleep tight, trusting him to fill in the missing pieces of your life.

Confidence

I am still confident of this:
    I will see the goodness of the LORD
    in the land of the living.

Psalm 27:13

The fruit of righteousness will be peace;
    the effect of righteousness will be quietness
        and confidence forever.

Isaiah 32:17

*In [Christ Jesus our Lord] and through faith
in him we may approach God with freedom
and confidence.*

Ephesians 3:12

For you have been my hope,
        O Sovereign LORD,
    my confidence since my youth.
From birth I have relied on you;
    you brought me forth from my
            mother's womb.
    I will ever praise you.

Psalm 71:5–6

Let us then approach the throne of grace with confidence, so that we may receive mercy and find grace to help us in our time of need.

Hebrews 4:16

I can do everything through [Christ] who gives me strength.

Philippians 4:13

Nothing is impossible with God.

Luke 1:37

God is our refuge and strength,
an ever-present help in trouble.
Therefore we will not fear, though the earth give way
and the mountains fall into the heart of the sea.

Psalm 46:1

Confidence

Surely God is my salvation;
    I will trust and not be afraid.
The LORD, the LORD, is my strength and
        my song;
    he has become my salvation.

Isaiah 12:2

*The Lord stood at my side and gave me
strength, so that through me the message might
be fully proclaimed.*

2 Timothy 4:17

The LORD gives strength to his people;
    the LORD blesses his people with peace.

Psalm 29:11

The Sovereign LORD is my strength;
    he makes my feet like the feet of a deer,
    he enables me to go on the heights.

Habakkuk 3:19

My flesh and my heart my fail,
    but God is the strength of my heart
    and my portion forever.

Psalm 73:26

One thing God has spoken,
   two things have I heard:
that you, O God, are strong,
   and that you, O Lord, are loving.

Psalm 62:11

Do not throw away your confidence; it will be richly rewarded. You need to persevere so that when you have done the will of God, you will receive what he has promised.

Hebrews 10:35–36

The LORD is my strength and my shield;
   my heart trusts in him, and I am helped.
My heart leaps for joy
   and I will give thanks to him in song.

Psalm 28:7

God is faithful; he will not let you be tempted beyond what you can bear. But when you are tempted, he will also provide a way out so that you can stand up under it.

1 Corinthians 10:13

Confidence

Those who hope in the LORD
   will renew their strength.
They will soar on wings like eagles;
   they will run and not grow weary,
   they will walk and not be faint.

Isaiah 40:31

Do not fear, for I am with you;
   do not be dismayed, for I am your God.
I will strengthen you and help you;
   I will uphold you with my righteous
      right hand.

Isaiah 41:10

The LORD is righteous in all his ways
   and loving toward all he has made.
The LORD is near to all who call on him,
   to all who call on him in truth.
He fulfills the desires of those who fear him;
   he hears their cry and saves them.

Psalm 145:17 – 19

your source of confidence

What do you rely upon to give you confidence?

When relying upon ourselves, we will not feel qualified for that to which God calls us. In fact, throughout Scripture we see that God often chooses people who felt unqualified for the tasks God laid before them. For example, Abraham, Moses, David, Esther and Mary. If God can use a roaming Bedouin to begin a new nation, a stuttering speaker to confront the Pharaoh of Egypt, a ruddy shepherd boy to lead Israel, an exiled Jewish girl to save her people and a timid teenage girl to bear the Son of God, then God can use us! The critical question isn't "Can I do this?" It's rather "Can God do this through me?"

So if you find yourself needing some confidence in a new situation today, trust God every step of the way. Stand not on your own fluctuating abilities but on the unchanging Rock, and nothing will shake your confidence.

Discernment

Wisdom is found on the lips of the discerning.

Proverbs 10:13

Praise be to the name of God for ever
and ever;
wisdom and power are his.
He changes times and seasons;
he sets up kings and deposes them.
He gives wisdom to the wise
and knowledge to the discerning.

Daniel 2:20–21

*Solomon said, "Now, O LORD my God, you have
made your servant king in place of my father
David. But I am only a little child and do not
know how to carry out my duties. So give your
servant a discerning heart to govern your people
and to distinguish between right and wrong."*

1 Kings 3:7, 9

Let us discern for ourselves what is right;
let us learn together what is good.

Job 34:4

And this is my prayer: that your love may abound more and more in knowledge and depth of insight, so that you may be able to discern what is best and may be pure and blameless until the day of Christ.

Philippians 1:9–10

Buy the truth and do not sell it;
    get wisdom, discipline and understanding.

Proverbs 23:23

The fear of the LORD is the beginning
        of wisdom;
    all who follow his precepts have
        good understanding.
    To him belongs eternal praise.

Psalm 111:10

I am your servant; give me discernment
    that I may understand your statutes.

Psalm 119:125

Discernment

The mocker seeks wisdom and finds none,
   but knowledge comes easily to the
      discerning.

Proverbs 14:6

Wisdom, like an inheritance, is a good thing
   and benefits those who see the sun.
Wisdom is a shelter
   as money is a shelter,
but the advantage of knowledge is this:
   that wisdom preserves the life of
      its possessor.

Ecclesiastes 7:11–12

A man's wisdom gives him patience;
   it is to his glory to overlook an offense.

Proverbs 19:11

*If any of you lacks wisdom, he should ask God,
who gives generously to all without finding fault,
and it will be given to him.*

James 1:5

Those who are wise will shine like the brightness of the heavens, and those who lead many to righteousness, like the stars for ever and ever.
Daniel 12:3

The wise in heart are called discerning,
and pleasant words promote instruction.
Proverbs 16:21

The heart of the discerning acquires
knowledge;
the ears of the wise seek it out.
Proverbs 18:15

The fear of the LORD is the beginning
of wisdom,
and knowledge of the Holy One is
understanding.
Proverbs 9:10

Let the wise listen and add to their learning,
and let the discerning get guidance.
Proverbs 1:5

Discernment

Who is wise and understanding among you? Let him show it by his good life, by deeds done in the humility that comes from wisdom.

James 3:13

He who walks with the wise grows wise,
    but a companion of fools suffers harm.

Proverbs 13:20

The wisdom that comes from heaven is first of all pure; then peace-loving, considerate, submissive, full of mercy and good fruit, impartial and sincere.

James 3:17–18

He who gets wisdom loves his own soul;
    he who cherishes understanding prospers.

Proverbs 19:8

Pride only breeds quarrels,
    but wisdom is found in those who
        take advice.

Proverbs 13:10

a discerning woman

He's gone and done it this time!"
Have you ever heard those words
coming from your lips? Perhaps you were
mumbling about your husband or your boss.
The situation you feared came true. Someone
with whom you live or work made a poor
decision with potentially disastrous results,
and you are facing the consequences. What
should you do?

Catherine Marshall said, "The purpose
of all prayer is to find God's will and to make
that will our prayer."

When you become aware of a crisis that
is escalating in your home or workplace, ask
God to give you the discernment to think
quickly and act decisively. Then intervene with
kindness on your lips and grace in your heart.
Be more concerned with what you can offer
than what you cannot offer. Use the resources
that God has placed at your disposal to
help find a peaceful solution to a possibly
explosive situation.

Faith

The LORD loves the just
and will not forsake his faithful ones.

Psalm 37:28

Jesus said, "Blessed are those who have not seen
and yet have believed."

John 20:29

It is by faith you stand firm.

2 Corinthians 1:24

Faith is being sure of what we hope for and certain
of what we do not see.

Hebrews 11:1

It is by grace you have been saved, through
faith—and this not from yourselves, it is the gift
of God—not by works, so that no one can boast.

Ephesians 2:8–9

Jesus said, "I tell you the truth, if you have faith as small as a mustard seed, you can say to this mountain, 'Move from here to there' and it will move. Nothing will be impossible for you."

Matthew 17:20

For in Christ Jesus ... the only thing that counts is faith expressing itself through love.

Galatians 5:6

Everyone born of God overcomes the world. This is the victory that has overcome the world, even our faith.

1 John 5:4

Faith

Since we have been justified through faith, we have peace with God through our Lord Jesus Christ.

Romans 5:1

Everything is possible for him who believes.

Mark 9:23

Take up the shield of faith, with which you can extinguish all the flaming arrows of the evil one.

Ephesians 6:16

I have fought the good fight, I have finished the race, I have kept the faith.

2 Timothy 4:7

I know your deeds, your love and faith, your service and perseverance, and that you are now doing more than you did at first.

Revelation 2:19

Yet to all who received him, to those who believed in his name, he gave the right to become children of God—children born not of natural descent, nor of human decision or a husband's will, but born of God.

John 1:12–13

Let us fix our eyes on Jesus, the author and perfecter of our faith.

Hebrews 12:2

We live by faith, not by sight.

2 Corinthians 5:7

Be on your guard; stand firm in the faith; ... be strong.

1 Corinthians 16:13

Faith

If you believe, you will receive whatever you ask for in prayer.

Matthew 21:22

If you confess with your mouth, "Jesus is Lord," and believe in your heart that God raised him from the dead, you will be saved.

Romans 10:9

nothing's impossible

"Faith sees the invisible, believes the unbelievable and receives the impossible." It may be easy to say these words when times are good. But these words were spoken by Corrie ten Boom while she suffered in a Nazi concentration camp. She knew that God would provide.

God is the same yesterday, today and forever. When Elijah found a hiding place with a widow and her son, their jar of flour and jug of oil never ran dry. God faithfully supplied them during their time of need.

What do you need from God? Is the paycheck barely enough to cover the bills? Do the clothes seem as though they won't last another season? Do you feel you can't handle another day in your present circumstances? God is able to provide everything you need to live. He will multiply his grace toward his people in their times of trouble. He sees you in your hiding place and will find a way to meet your needs.

Fear

Jesus said, "Don't be afraid; just believe."

Mark 5:36

I sought the LORD, and he answered me;
   he delivered me from all my fears.

Psalm 34:4

I am the LORD, your God,
   who takes hold of your right hand
and says to you, Do not fear;
   I will help you.

Isaiah 41:13

Do not be afraid; do not be discouraged. Be strong and courageous.

Joshua 10:25

There is no fear in love. But perfect love drives out fear.

1 John 4:18

The Lord is my helper; I will not be afraid.

Hebrews 13:6

If God is for us, who can be against us?

Romans 8:31

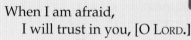

Jesus said, "Peace I leave with you; my peace I give you. I do not give to you as the world gives. Do not let your hearts be troubled and do not be afraid."

John 14:27

When I am afraid,
   I will trust in you, [O LORD.]

Psalm 56:3

Do not be afraid or discouraged, for the LORD God, my God, is with you. He will not fail you or forsake you.

1 Chronicles 28:20

Even though I walk
   through the valley of the shadow of death,
I will fear no evil;
   for you are with me;
your rod and your staff,
   they comfort me.

Psalm 23:4

Fear

Strengthen the feeble hands,
    steady the knees that give way;
say to those with fearful hearts,
    "Be strong, do not fear;
your God will come,
    he will come with vengeance;
with divine retribution
    he will come to save you."

Isaiah 35:3–4

You will go on your way in safety,
    and your foot will not stumble;
when you lie down, you will not be afraid;
    when you lie down, your sleep will
        be sweet.
Have no fear of sudden disaster
    or of the ruin that overtakes the wicked,
for the Lord will be your confidence
    and will keep your foot from being snared.

Proverbs 3:23–26

walking unafraid

Sometimes we fear people who may do us harm—those in authority may fire us or those who dislike us may injure our reputation. We may violate our own consciences so we don't offend those who make sure their opinions are heard. But when we fear what people will think, we become ruled by changing whims and fashions. We are ruled more by our self-interest and our fears than by our love for others or for God.

God promises that even if our boss fires us, our best friend gossips behind our back or our teenager rolls her eyes when we insist on godly standards, God will surround us and protect us.

David, who wrote Psalm 27, was unafraid because he knew God was his light and salvation. He put his complete trust in God and walked with confidence in the face of dangerous enemies. Today our world keeps getting darker and darker. But with God as your stronghold, you can walk unafraid in this world.

Forgiveness

*If we confess our sins, [God] is faithful and just
and will forgive us our sins and purify us from all
unrighteousness.*

1 John 1:9

*[God] has rescued us from the dominion of
darkness and brought us into the kingdom of the
Son he loves, in whom we have redemption, the
forgiveness of sins.*

Colossians 1:13 – 14

*We do not make requests of you because we are
righteous, but because of your great mercy. O
Lord, listen! O Lord, forgive! O Lord, hear and
act! For your sake, O my God, do not delay.*

Daniel 9:18 – 19

"Come now, let us reason together,"
    says the LORD.
"Though your sins are like scarlet,
    they shall be as white as snow;
though they are red as crimson,
    they shall be like wool."

Isaiah 1:18

*The Lord our God is merciful
and forgiving, even though we
have rebelled against him.*

Daniel 9:9

*In [Christ] we have
redemption through his blood,
the forgiveness of sins, in
accordance with the riches of God's grace.*

Ephesians 1:7

Help us, O God our Savior,
    for the glory of your name;
deliver us and forgive our sins
    for your name's sake.

Psalm 79:9

Blessed are they
    whose transgressions are forgiven,
    whose sins are covered.
Blessed is the man
    whose sin the Lord will never count
        against him.

Romans 4:7 – 8

Forgiveness

The Lord is compassionate and gracious,
  slow to anger, abounding in love.
He will not always accuse,
  nor will he harbor his anger forever;
he does not treat us as our sins deserve
  or repay us according to our iniquities.
For as high as the heavens are above the earth,
  so great is his love for those who fear him;
as far as the east is from the west,
  so far has he removed our transgressions
    from us.

Psalm 103:8–12

Bear with each other and forgive whatever
grievances you may have against one another.
Forgive as the Lord forgave you.

Colossians 3:13

I am the Lord, your Holy One,
  Israel's Creator, your King.
I, even I, am he who blots out
  your transgressions, for my own sake,
  and remembers your sins no more.

Isaiah 43:15, 25

*The LORD, the LORD, the
compassionate and gracious
God, slow to anger, abounding
in love and faithfulness,
maintaining love to thousands,
and forgiving wickedness,
rebellion and sin.*

Exodus 34:6–7

*Repent, then, and turn to God, so that your sins
may be wiped out, that times of refreshing may
come from the Lord.*

Acts 3:19

Praise the LORD, O my soul,
    and forget not all his benefits—
who forgives all your sins
    and heals all your diseases.

Psalm 103:2–3

*You are a forgiving God, gracious and
compassionate, slow to anger and abounding
in love.*

Nehemiah 9:17

Forgiveness

If you, O LORD, kept a record of sins,
    O Lord, who could stand?
But with you there is forgiveness;
    therefore you are feared.

Psalm 130:3–4

Who is a God like you,
    who pardons sin and forgives the
        transgression
    of the remnant of his inheritance?
You do not stay angry forever
    but delight to show mercy.

Micah 7:18

In your love you kept me
    from the pit of destruction;
you have put all my sins
    behind your back.

Isaiah 38:17

Jesus said, "If you forgive men when they sin against you, your heavenly Father will also forgive you."

Matthew 6:14

total forgiveness

Is there any sin God won't forgive? Maybe you think he won't forgive abortion. Maybe you think he won't forgive adultery. Or abandonment. Or alcoholism. Or abuse. And those are just the "A's." But God's forgiveness encompasses the whole alphabet—A to Z. Jesus Christ paid for that forgiveness long ago—with his life.

You may not feel forgiven. You may even feel guilty about your past sins. But you need to know that if you have confessed your sins to God, he has really, really forgiven you. God is not like human beings who hold grudges or cling to bitterness. Once he forgives, he chooses to forget.

Is there something nagging at your conscience that you think God hasn't forgiven? Confess it once and for all. Leave it in the hands of Jesus. God has forgiven it. Now it is your choice to walk like you are forgiven and act like you are forgiven. One day you will even feel like you are forgiven.

Giving Thanks

Thanks be to God! He gives us the victory through our Lord Jesus Christ.

1 Corinthians 15:57

Give thanks to the LORD for his unfailing love.

Psalm 107:21

Just as you received Christ Jesus as Lord, continue to live in him, rooted and built up in him, strengthened in the faith as you were taught, and overflowing with thanksgiving.

Colossians 2:6−7

Praise the LORD.
How good it is to sing praises to our God,
    how pleasant and fitting to praise him.
Sing to the LORD with thanksgiving.

Psalm 147:1, 7

And whatever you do, whether in word or deed, do it all in the name of the Lord Jesus, giving thanks to God the Father through him.

Colossians 3:17

Be filled with the Spirit. Speak to one another with psalms, hymns and spiritual songs. Sing and make music in your heart to the Lord, always giving thanks to God the Father for everything, in the name of our Lord Jesus Christ.

Ephesians 5:18–20

Give thanks to the LORD, call on his name;
    make known among the nations what
       he has done.
Sing to him, sing praise to him;
    tell of all his wonderful acts.

1 Chronicles 16:8–9

You are my God, and I will give you thanks;
    you are my God, and I will exalt you.
Give thanks to the LORD, for he is good;
    his love endures forever.

Psalm 118:28–29

Giving Thanks

Come, let us sing for joy to the LORD;
   let us shout aloud to the Rock of
      our salvation.
Let us come before him with thanksgiving;
   and extol him with music and song.

Psalm 95:1–2

*We know that the one who raised the Lord
Jesus from the dead will also raise us with Jesus
and present us with you in his presence. All
this is for your benefit, so that the grace that
is reaching more and more people may cause
thanksgiving to overflow to the glory of God.*

2 Corinthians 4:14–15

*Everything God created is good, and nothing is
to be rejected if it is received with thanksgiving,
because it is consecrated by the word of God
and prayer.*

1 Timothy 4:4–5

everyday give thanks

Happy Thanksgiving Day! You say today isn't Thanksgiving? Maybe it isn't even the right month? You're certain of that because there's no turkey roasting in the oven and no pumpkin pie baking.

Let's forget the calendar and the menus and get ready to give thanks. Times of thanksgiving need not be reserved for momentous occasions. Consider the countless reasons you have to be grateful. Has something brought great joy to your life? If not today, how about yesterday? Or last week? Or last month? Consider those small things we so easily take for granted.

Today is the perfect time to count your blessings, then "give thanks to the LORD, for he is good."

God's Love

This is how God showed his love among us: He sent his one and only Son into the world that we might live through him. This is love: not that we loved God, but that he loved us and sent his Son as an atoning sacrifice for our sins.

1 John 4:9–10

May your unfailing love come to me, O LORD,
   your salvation according to your promise.

Psalm 119:41

Praise be to the LORD,
   for he showed his wonderful love to me.

Psalm 31:21

I will sing of your strength,
   in the morning I will sing of your love;
for you are my fortress,
   my refuge in times of trouble.

Psalm 59:16

Jesus said, "The Father himself loves you because you have loved me and have believed that I came from God."

John 16:27

*Who shall separate us from the
love of Christ? Shall trouble
or hardship or persecution
or famine or nakedness or
danger or sword? No, in all
these things we are more than
conquerors through him who
loved us.*

Romans 8:35, 37

How priceless is your unfailing love,
    [O LORD!]
Both high and low among men
    find refuge in the shadow of your wings.

Psalm 36:7

*I am convinced that neither death nor life, neither
angel nor demons, neither the present nor the
future, nor any powers, neither height nor depth,
nor anything else in all creation, will be able to
separate us from the love of God that is in Christ
Jesus our Lord.*

Romans 8:38–39

God's Love

Dear friends, since God so loved us, we also ought to love one another. No one has ever seen God; but if we love one another, God lives in us and his love is made complete in us.

1 John 4:11–12

Keep yourselves in God's love as you wait for the mercy of our Lord Jesus Christ to bring you to eternal life.

Jude v.21

If anyone acknowledges that Jesus is the Son of God, God lives in him and he in God. And so we know and rely on the love God has for us. God is love. Whoever lives in love lives in God, and God in him.

1 John 4:15–16

Because of his great love for us, God, who is rich in mercy, made us alive with Christ even when we were dead in transgressions—it is by grace you have been saved.

Ephesians 2:4–5

Hope does not disappoint us,
because God has poured out
his love into our hearts by
the Holy Spirit, whom he has
given us. God demonstrates
his own love for us in this:
While we were still sinners, Christ died for us.

Romans 5:5, 8

O my Strength, I sing praise to you,
   you, O God, are my fortress, my
         loving God.

Psalm 59:17

[God] sends from heaven and saves me....
   God sends his love and his faithfulness.

Psalm 57:3

You are forgiving and good, O Lord,
   abounding in love to all who call to you.

Psalm 86:5

God's Love

I will sing of the LORD's great love forever;
  with my mouth I will make your
    faithfulness known through
    all generations.
I will declare that your love stands
    firm forever,
  that you established your faithfulness
    in heaven itself.

Psalm 89:1–2

Because of the LORD's great love we are
    not consumed,
  for his compassions never fail.
They are new every morning;
  great is your faithfulness.

Lamentations 3:22–23

God so loved the world that he gave his one and only Son, that whoever believes in him shall not perish but have eternal life.

John 3:16

endearing love endures

God not only offers you enduring love, he also extends to you endearing love. This describes a strong affection that lifts one higher or increases the value of the one beloved. Enduring speaks of the quantity of God's love while endearing portrays the quality.

God loved us before we were lovely. We are his diamonds in the rough. In the rough, a diamond looks like a common pebble. But the stone must undergo a finishing process to bring out its full radiance. The gem is held against a large grinding wheel to cut and polish the stone. If the diamond is intended for someone prominent, many meticulous hours are spent perfecting it.

God has lifted you out of the rubble of a worthless life. He has polished and chiseled you into a jewel of great beauty. You are his diamond meant to enjoy his love forever.

God's Plan

"I know the plans I have for you," declares the LORD, "plans to prosper you and not to harm you, plans to give you hope and a future."

Jeremiah 29:11

It is God who works in you to will and to act according to his good purpose.

Philippians 2:13

I know that you can do all things;
   no plan of yours can be thwarted.

Job 42:1–2

O LORD, you are my God;
   I will exalt you and praise your name,
for in perfect faithfulness
   you have done marvelous things,
   things planned long ago.

Isaiah 25:1

The LORD will fulfill his purpose for me;
   your love, O LORD, endures forever—
   do not abandon the works of your hands.

Psalm 138:8

In [Christ] we were also chosen, having been predestined according to the plan of him who works out everything in conformity with the purpose of his will, in order that we, who were the first to hope in Christ, might be for the praise of his glory.

Ephesians 1:11

I am God, and there is no other;
    I am God, and there is none like me.
I make known the end from the beginning,
    from ancient times, what is still to come.
I say: My purpose will stand,
    and I will do all that I please.
From the east I summon a bird of prey;
    from a far-off land, a man to fulfill
        my purpose.
What I have said, that will I bring about;
    what I have planned, that will I do.

Isaiah 46:9–11

God's Plan

I cry out to God Most High,
to God, who fulfills his purpose for me.

Psalm 57:2

The plans of the LORD stand firm forever,
the purposes of his heart through
all generations.

Psalm 33:11

In his heart a man plans his course,
but the LORD determines his steps.

Proverbs 16:9

*We know that in all things God works for the
good of those who love him, who have been called
according to his purpose.*

Romans 8:28

Many, O LORD my God,
are the wonders you have done.
The things you planned for us
no one can recount to you;
were I to speak and tell of them,
they would be too many to declare.

Psalm 40:5

God has big plans

God has big plans for you. He has
transformed your heart into a temple for
his Holy Spirit. In this day and age it takes
courage to be a godly woman. There will
be people who oppose God's work in your
life. There will be naysayers who may try to
convince you that the cost of serving God is
too high or that the time and attention you pay
to his Word is too great. There will be those
who say you can cut corners and disregard
God's blueprint for your life.

Don't believe it. The same God who
helped David fight giants is the same God
who enabled Solomon to build the most
magnificent temple known to man. That
God is your God and he inhabits your heart.
God was faithful to stay with Solomon and
complete the work of the temple. He will be
faithful to complete the good work he began
in you, too.

God's Power

Be strong in the Lord and in his mighty power.

Ephesians 6:10

I pray that you may know [God's] incomparably great power for us who believe. That power is like the working of his mighty strength, which he exerted in Christ when he raised him from the dead and seated him at his right hand in the heavenly realms.

Ephesians 1:18–20

Jesus said to me, "My grace is sufficient for you, for my power is made perfect in weakness." Therefore I will boast all the more gladly about my weaknesses, so that Christ's power may rest on me.

2 Corinthians 12:9

[Abraham] did not waver through unbelief regarding the promise of God, but was strengthened in his faith and gave glory to God, being fully persuaded that God had power to do what he had promised.

Romans 4:20–21

*Jesus said, "I will remain
in the world no longer, but
[my followers] are still in
the world, and I am coming
to you. Holy Father, protect
them by the power of your
name—the name you gave
me—so that they may be one
as we are one."*

John 17:11

Great is our Lord and mighty in power;
   his understanding has no limit.

Psalm 147:5

Do you not know?
   Have you not heard?
The LORD is the everlasting God,
   the Creator of the ends of the earth.
He will not grow tired or weary,
   and his understanding no one can fathom.
He gives strength to the weary
   and increases the power of the weak.

Isaiah 40:28–29

God's Power

You are awesome, O God, in your sanctuary;
the God of Israel gives power and strength
to his people.
Praise be to God!

Psalm 68:35

*Ah, Sovereign LORD, you have made the heavens
and the earth by your great power and outstretched
arm. Nothing is too hard for you.*

Jeremiah 32:17

*I pray that out of [God's] glorious riches he may
strengthen you with power through his Spirit in
your inner being, so that Christ may dwell in your
hearts through faith.*

Ephesians 3:16 – 17

*Now to [God] who is able to do immeasurably
more than all we ask or imagine, according to his
power that is at work within us, to him be glory
in the church and in Christ Jesus throughout all
generations, for ever and ever! Amen.*

Ephesians 3:20 – 21

*[Christ's] divine power has
given us everything we need
for life and godliness through
our knowledge of him who
called us by his own glory
and goodness. Through these
he has given us his very great
and precious promises, so that
through them you may participate in the divine
nature and escape the corruption in the world
caused by evil desires.*

2 Peter 1:3–4

Yours, O Lord, is the greatness and the power
   and the glory and the majesty and
       the splendor,
   for everything in heaven and earth
      is yours.
Yours, O Lord, is the kingdom;
   you are exalted as head over all.

1 Chronicles 29:11

God's Power

The angel answered [Mary], "The Holy Spirit will come upon you, and the power of the Most High will overshadow you. So the holy one to be born will be called the Son of God."

Luke 1:35

God made the earth by his power;
    he founded the world by his wisdom
    and stretched out the heavens by
        his understanding.

Jeremiah 10:12

[God] rules forever by his power,
    his eyes watch the nations—
    let not the rebellious rise up against him.

Psalm 66:7

Jesus said, "With God all things are possible."

Matthew 19:26

"I have raised you up for this very purpose, that I might show you my power and that my name might be proclaimed in all the earth," says the LORD.

Exodus 9:16

Jesus said, "You will receive power when the Holy Spirit comes on you; and you will be my witnesses in Jerusalem, and in all Judea and Samaria, and to the ends of the earth."

Acts 1:8

Great is our Lord and mighty in power;
   his understanding has no limit.

Psalm 147:5

I heard what sounded like the roar of a great multitude in heaven shouting:
"Hallelujah!
Salvation and glory and power belong to
      our God,
   for true and just are his judgments."

Revelation 19:1–2

Your ways, O God, are holy.
   What god is so great as our God?
You are the God who performs miracles;
   you display your power among
      the peoples.

Psalm 77:13–14

God's Power

Say to God, "How awesome are your deeds!
  So great is your power
  that your enemies cringe before you.
All the earth bows down to you;
  they sing praise to you,
  they sing praise to your name."

Psalm 66:3–4

*We pray . . . that you may live a life worthy of
the Lord and may please him in every way:
bearing fruit in every good work, growing in the
knowledge of God, being strengthened with all
power according to his glorious might so that you
may have great endurance and patience.*

Colossians 1:10–11

*O LORD, God of our fathers, are you not the God
who is in heaven? You rule over all the kingdoms
of the nations. Power and might are in your hand,
and no one can withstand you.*

2 Chronicles 20:6

the power of the weak

The story of David and Goliath illustrates how God delights in calling out those who are small and insignificant. It's a picture of God covering his people with strength and power; equipping them to accomplish amazing things for his good purpose. We see God empowering the weak to conquer the strong demonstrated throughout the Bible: Moses standing before Pharaoh, Elijah standing against the prophets of Baal, and Deborah fighting Sisera's army. When we look around in our churches, we see the same thing happening today. Pastors equipped with God's Word are fighting for souls from the pulpit. Sunday school teachers sing songs to gain ground over young children's hearts. Women hold prayer meetings to battle for their families and marriages.

The time has come to move from defense to offense, to come against the seeming giants. Don the armor of God ... then, when the giants try to intimidate you, pick out your pebble of faith and take aim.

God's Word

Let the word of Christ dwell in you richly as you teach and admonish one another with all wisdom, and as you sing psalms, hymns and spiritual songs with gratitude in your hearts to God.

Colossians 3:16

The grass withers and the flowers fall,
   but the word of our God stands forever.

Isaiah 40:8

All Scripture is God-breathed and is useful for teaching, rebuking, correcting and training in righteousness.

2 Timothy 3:16

The word of God is living and active. Sharper than any double-edged sword, it penetrates even to dividing soul and spirit, joints and marrow; it judges the thoughts and attitudes of the heart.

Hebrews 4:12

Man does not live on bread alone but on every word that comes from the mouth of the LORD.

Deuteronomy 8:3

*Fix these words of mine in
your hearts and minds; tie
them as symbols on your
hands and bind them on your
foreheads. Teach them to your
children, talking about them
when you sit at home and
when you walk along the road,
when you lie down and when you get up.*

Deuteronomy 11:18–19

Your word is a lamp to my feet
    and a light for my path.

Psalm 119:105

*In the beginning was the Word, and the Word
was with God, and the Word was God.*

John 1:1

I have hidden your word in my heart
    that I might not sin against you.
Praise be to you, O LORD;
    teach me your decrees.

Psalm 119:11–12

God's Word

Jesus said, *"Everyone who hears these words of mine and puts them into practice is like a wise man who built his house on the rock. The rain came down, the streams rose, and the winds blew and beat against that house; yet it did not fall, because it had its foundation on the rock."*

Matthew 7:24

"As the rain and the snow
   come down from heaven,
and do not return to it
   without watering the earth
and making it bud and flourish,
   so that it yields seed for the sower and
      bread for the eater,
so is my word that goes out from my mouth:
   It will not return to me empty,
but will accomplish what I desire
   and achieve the purpose for which I
      sent it,"
declares the Lord.

Isaiah 55:10–11

home improvement

True home improvement does not begin with the exterior but the interior. It starts with heart improvement. So God commanded the Israelites to pass on his holy commands, decrees and laws to their children through their lives and thoughts. God commanded his Word to surround them like a blanket and sustain them like home-baked bread. Only God's Word can do the work of improving the lives of his people, generation to generation.

God doesn't want his principles displayed outwardly if they don't impact us inwardly—on our hearts and souls and minds. When his principles are ingrained on our inmost being, they will change the way we think, act and live.

Are you spending so much time on outward home decorating that you've neglected inward home improvement? Take the time to memorize Scripture, read the Bible and tell your kids and your kids' kids about God. That kind of home improvement is eternal.

Grief

All my longings lie open before you, O Lord;
　　my sighing is not hidden from you.

Psalm 38:9

For men are not cast off
　　by the Lord forever.
Though he brings grief, he will show
　　　　compassion,
　　so great is his unfailing love.
For he does not willingly bring affliction
　　or grief to the children of men.

Lamentations 3:31 – 33

Give ear to my words, O Lord,
　　consider my sighing.
Listen to my cry for help,
　　my King and my God,
　　for to you I pray.

Psalm 5:1 – 2

Be strong and take heart,
　　all you who hope in the Lord.

Psalm 31:24

We do not want you to be ignorant about those who fall asleep, or to grieve like the rest of men, who have no hope. We believe that Jesus died and rose again and so we believe that God will bring with Jesus those who have fallen asleep in him.

1 Thessalonians 4:13–14

May our Lord Jesus Christ himself and God our Father, who loved us and by his grace gave us eternal encouragement and good hope, encourage your hearts and strengthen you in every good deed and word.

2 Thessalonians 2:16–17

Why are you downcast, O my soul?
    Why so disturbed within me?
Put your hope in God,
    for I will yet praise him,
    my Savior and my God.

Psalm 42:11

Grief

We who have fled to take hold of the hope offered to us may be greatly encouraged. We have this hope as an anchor for the soul, firm and secure.

Be merciful to me, O Lᴏʀᴅ, for I am in distress;
   my eyes grow weak with sorrow,
   my soul and my body with grief.

Psalm 31:9

Jesus said, "I tell you the truth, you will weep and mourn while the world rejoices. You will grieve, but your grief will turn to joy."

John 16:20

Let us then approach the throne of grace with confidence, so that we may receive mercy and find grace to help us in our time of need.

Hebrews 4:16

"I will turn their mourning into gladness;
   I will give them comfort and joy instead
      of sorrow," says the Lᴏʀᴅ.

Jeremiah 31:13

"I, even I, am he who comforts you,"
says the LORD.

Isaiah 51:12

We are hard pressed on every side, but not crushed; perplexed, but not in despair; persecuted, but not abandoned; struck down, but not destroyed. Therefore we do not lose heart. Though outwardly we are wasting away, yet inwardly we are being renewed day by day. So we fix our eyes not on what is seen, but on what is unseen. For what is seen is temporary, but what is unseen is eternal.

2 Corinthians 4:8, 16, 18

I heard a loud voice from the throne saying, "Now the dwelling of God is with men, and he will live with them. They will be his people, and God himself will be with them and be their God. He will wipe every tear from their eyes. There will be no more death or mourning or crying or pain, for the old order of things has passed away."

Revelation 21:3–4

101

Grief

Shout for joy, O heavens;
    rejoice, O earth;
    burst into song, O mountains!
For the Lord comforts his people
    and will have compassion on his
       afflicted ones.

Isaiah 49:13

Jesus said, " In this world you will have trouble.
But take heart! I have overcome the world."

John 16:33

Jesus said, "Come to me, all you who are weary
and burdened, and I will give you rest. Take my
yoke upon you and learn from me, for I am gentle
and humble in heart, and you will find rest for
your souls."

Matthew 11:28–29

You, O Lord, keep my lamp burning;
    my God turns my darkness into light.

Psalm 18:28

comfort in grief

Have you ever tried to comfort someone who refused to be comforted? We've all seen or experienced the gut-wrenching sorrow where we want to cover our faces and turn back the hands of time. Sometimes all we can do is utter the name of the person we've lost.

There are other types of losses worth grieving: the death of a marriage, a friendship or your health. Then comes the anguish where you want to blank out the present, look to the past and repeat the name as if it might reverse what happened. In the freshness of the pain, it might seem you can never again function.

Maybe you are overwhelmed by a devastating grief right now or are trying to encourage someone else in a similar situation. Embrace your personal grief, but remember: God has not promised immunity from sorrow; but he has promised that he will walk with us through it.

Guilt

Let us draw near to God with a sincere heart in full assurance of faith, having our hearts sprinkled to cleanse us from a guilty conscience and having our bodies washed with pure water.

Hebrews 10:22

Have mercy on me, O God,
  according to your unfailing love;
according to your great compassion
  blot out my transgressions.
Wash away all my iniquity
  and cleanse me from my sin.

Psalm 51:1–2

All have sinned and fall short of the glory of God, and are justified freely by his grace through the redemption that came by Christ Jesus.

Romans 3:23–24

I said, "I will confess
  my transgressions to the LORD"—
and you forgave
  the guilt of my sin.

Psalm 32:5

enough guilt

In the Old Testament sacrifices were considered a symbolic gesture foreshadowing the ultimate sacrifice, Jesus Christ. When Jesus offered himself on the cross, he paid the debt of sin in full. He declared his followers, "Not guilty." The law was fulfilled. No other blood sacrifice will ever be required.

We feel guilty enough! We feel guilty if we work, guilty if we don't, guilty for not spending enough time with our husband, kids and friends, and guilty for not taking time for God and ourselves. Thankfully Jesus declared from the cross, "Not guilty." We can live guilt free while making personal offerings: repentance of sin, praise to God and service to others—sacrifices pleasing to God.

We've all sinned. Christ purchased forgiveness on the cross. Offer him the sacrifice of confession and you'll be cleansed. Then pour out the sacrifice of praise; he's worthy of all honor. Present the sacrifice of service: When you help others in God's name, you'll discover you're the one who benefits.

Happiness

A happy heart makes the face cheerful.

Proverbs 15:13

Is anyone happy? Let him sing songs of praise.

James 5:13

May the righteous be glad
    and rejoice before God;
    may they be happy and joyful.

Psalm 68:3

*A man can do nothing better than to eat and drink
and find satisfaction in his work. This too, I see,
is from the hand of God, for without him, who can
eat or find enjoyment? To the man who pleases
him, God gives wisdom, knowledge and happiness.*

Ecclesiastes 2:24 – 26

When times are good, be happy;
    but when times are bad, consider:
God has made the one
    as well as the other.

Ecclesiastes 7:14

When God gives any man wealth and possessions, and enables him to enjoy them, to accept his lot and be happy in his work—this is a gift of God. He seldom reflects on the days of his life, because God keeps him occupied with gladness of heart.

Ecclesiastes 5:19–20

This is the day the LORD has made,
    let us rejoice and be glad in it.

Psalm 118:24

Go, eat your food with gladness, and drink your wine with a joyful heart, for it is now that God favors what you do.

Ecclesiastes 9:7

Happiness

You make me glad by your deeds, O LORD;
   I sing for joy at the works of your hands.

There is a time for everything,
   and a season for every activity
         under heaven:
a time to weep and a time to laugh,
a time to mourn and a time to dance.

I saw the Lord always before me,
Because he is at my right hand,
I will not be shaken.
Therefore my heart is glad and my
         tongue rejoices;
   my body also will live in hope.

oh, how happy!

Have you ever tried to catch the wind? Wind is illusive. It is non-tangible. Chimes or catchers hanging on your back porch may detect its presence or point out its direction. But they'll never contain it.

Securing happiness in life is like trying to catch the wind. We won't often find it in direct pursuit; it will always remain just out of reach. However, more than likely, the happiness we're searching for is waiting right there in our own backyard. True happiness is not having what you want, but wanting what you already have. Appreciating the present rather than pining for whatever the future may hold brings contentment.

The Bible uses the word *blessed*, which means "oh, how happy." To God, blessed people are happy people and happy people are blessed. The true source of pleasure is God. Don't try to catch the wind; instead lay hold of the wind Maker. In his presence are pleasures forevermore.

Honesty

May the words of my mouth and the
       meditation of my heart
be pleasing in your sight,
O Lord, my Rock and my Redeemer.

Psalm 19:14

*Speaking the truth in love, we will in all things
grow up into him who is the Head, that is, Christ.*

Ephesians 4:15

*I know, my God, that you test the heart and are
pleased with integrity.*

1 Chronicles 29:17

*I strive always to keep my conscience clear before
God and man.*

Acts 24:16

Kings take pleasure in honest lips;
    they value a man who speaks the truth.

Proverbs 16:13

Whatever is true, whatever is noble, whatever is right, whatever is pure, whatever is lovely, whatever is admirable—if anything is excellent or praiseworthy—think about such things.

Philippians 4:8

Show me your ways, O Lord,
    teach me your paths;
guide me in your truth and teach me,
    for you are God my Savior,
    and my hope is in you all day long.

Psalm 25:4–5

Whoever can be trusted with very little can also be trusted with much.

Luke 16:10

111

Honesty

Come, my children, listen to me;
    I will teach you the fear of the Lord.
Whoever of you loves life
    and desires to see many good days,
keep your tongue from evil
    and your lips from speaking lies.

Psalm 34:11 – 13

A truthful witness gives honest testimony,
    but a false witness tells lies.

Proverbs 12:17

Truthful lips endure forever,
    but a lying tongue lasts only a moment.
There is deceit in the hearts of those who
            plot evil,
    but joy for those who promote peace.
No harm befalls the righteous,
    but the wicked have their fill of trouble.
The Lord detests lying lips,
    but he delights in men who are truthful.

Proverbs 12:19 – 22

In your teaching show integrity, seriousness and soundness of speech that cannot be condemned.

Titus 2:7–8

Do not lie to each other, since you have taken off your old self with its practices and have put on the new self, which is being renewed in knowledge in the image of its Creator.

Colossians 3:9

Let us not become weary in doing good, for at the proper time we will reap a harvest if we do not give up.

Galatians 6:9

He who guards his mouth and his tongue keeps himself from calamity.

Proverbs 21:23

Honesty

Do your best to present yourself to God as one approved, a workman who does not need to be ashamed and who correctly handles the word of truth.

2 Timothy 2:15

If anyone speaks, he should do it as one speaking the very words of God.

1 Peter 4:11

Do not let any unwholesome talk come out of your mouths.

Ephesians 4:29

complete honesty

Honesty is the best policy. Most of us would agree with that statement. But let's add one more word to the statement: Complete honesty is the best policy. How does that change things? Is it possible we agree with the revised statement in theory but not in practice? Do we sometimes look for ways to compromise the truth to suit our purposes?

Even our white lies can open the door to compromise and sin. Maybe you don't tell the whole truth about the grocery money. Or you take home company supplies—after all, sometimes you work at home. But God will call for an accounting, and we will be asked to explain ourselves. And you might lose the trust of those you value most. How much better to live like the straightforward workers on the temple in 2 Kings 12. Their reputation for "complete honesty" went before them, gaining them the respect of their superiors and even the king. Complete honesty leaves no room for lies—big, little, black, white, or otherwise.

Identity

How great is the love the Father has lavished on us, that we should be called children of God! And that is what we are!

1 John 3:1

In [God] we live and move and have our being.

Acts 17:28

We are God's workmanship, created in Christ Jesus to do good works, which God prepared in advance for us to do.

Ephesians 2:10

The LORD your God is with you,
    he is mighty to save.
He will take great delight in you,
    he will quiet you with his love,
    he will rejoice over you with singing.

Zephaniah 3:17

If we live, we live to the Lord; and if we die, we die to the Lord. So, whether we live or die, we belong to the Lord.

Romans 14:8

Jesus said, "Are not five sparrows sold for two pennies? Yet not one of them is forgotten by God. Indeed, the very hairs of your head are all numbered. Don't be afraid; you are worth more than many sparrows."

Luke 12:6–7

Jesus said, "I am the vine; you are the branches. If a man remains in me and I in him, he will bear much fruit; apart from me you can do nothing. This is to my Father's glory, that you bear much fruit, showing yourselves to be my disciples."

John 15:5, 8

You created my inmost being;
    you knit me together in my mother's
        womb.
I praise you because I am fearfully and
        wonderfully made;
    your works are wonderful,
    I know that full well.

Psalm 139:13–14

Identity

You are the body of Christ, and each one of you is a part of it.

1 Corinthians 12:27

The LORD does not look at the things man looks at. Man looks at the outward appearance, but the LORD looks at the heart.

1 Samuel 16:7

Know that the LORD is God.
   It is he who made us, and we are his;
   we are his people, the sheep of his pasture.

Psalm 100:3

Those who are considered worthy of taking part ... in the resurrection from the dead ... can no longer die; for they are like the angels. They are God's children, since they are children of the resurrection.

Luke 20:35–36

"I will be a Father to you,
   and you will be my sons and daughters,"
      says the Lord Almighty.

2 Corinthians 6:18

This is what the LORD says—
Fear not, for I have redeemed you;
 I have summoned you by name; you
  are mine.

Isaiah 43:1

*When God created man, he made him in the
likeness of God. He created them male and female
and blessed them.*

Genesis 5:1–2

What is man that you are mindful of him,
 the son of man that you care for him?
You made him a little lower than the
  heavenly beings
 and crowned him with glory and honor.
You made him ruler over the works of
  your hands;
 you put everything under his feet.

Psalm 8:4–6

*When Christ, who is your life, appears, then you
also will appear with him in glory.*

Colossians 3:4

Identity

*The Spirit himself testifies with our spirit that we
are God's children. Now if we are children, then we
are heirs—heirs of God and co-heirs with Christ,
if indeed we share in his sufferings in order that
we may also share in his glory.*

Romans 8:16–17

This is what the LORD says:
"See, I have engraved you on the palms
of my hands."

Isaiah 49:8, 16

*We are the temple of the living God. As God
has said: "I will live with them and walk among
them, and I will be their God, and they will be
my people."*

2 Corinthians 6:16

*If anyone is in Christ, he is a new creation; the
old has gone, the new has come! We are therefore
Christ's ambassadors, as though God were making
his appeal through us.*

2 Corinthians 5:17, 20

a sense of identity

Our name reflects who we are. It gives us a sense of belonging, a sense of identity. If someone knows our name, it means they know *us.* It's hard not to take it personally when someone forgets our name. Unfortunately, parents do it. Bosses do it. Teachers do it. But if our closest friends, or boyfriend or husband forgot our name—it would be an almost unforgivable offense.

Thankfully, Jesus knows our name. The Creator of the universe, the One who determined the number of stars in the sky and called each of them by name, knows *your* name. Not only does he know your name, he calls you by name.

When you were saved, God spoke to you personally. And throughout your life, he calls your name as he leads you beside still waters, through the mountaintops and valleys of life, leading you to safe pastures as a shepherd guides his precious sheep.

Joy

Gladness and joy will overtake them,
    and sorrow and sighing will flee away.

Isaiah 35:10

Satisfy us in the morning with your
    unfailing love,
    that we may sing for joy and be glad all
    our days.

Psalm 90:14

A cheerful look brings joy to the heart,
    and good news gives health to the bones.

Proverbs 15:30

_Rejoice in the Lord always. I will say it again:
Rejoice!_

Philippians 4:4

_For the kingdom of God is not a matter of eating
and drinking, but of righteousness, peace and joy
in the Holy Spirit._

Romans 14:17

You have made known to
  me the path of life;
you will fill me with joy
  in your presence,
with eternal pleasures at
  your right hand.

Psalm 16:11

Weeping may remain for a night,
  but rejoicing comes in the morning.

Psalm 30:5

Those who sow in tears
  will reap with songs of joy.

Psalm 126:5

With joy you will draw water
  from the wells of salvation.

Isaiah 12:3

*Though you have not seen [Jesus,] you love him;
and even though you do not see him now, you
believe in him and are filled with an inexpressible
and glorious joy.*

1 Peter 1:8

Joy

Shout for joy to the LORD, all the earth.
  Worship the LORD with gladness;
  come before him with joyful songs.

Psalm 100:1–2

Do not grieve, for the joy of the LORD is your strength.

Nehemiah 8:10

May the God of hope fill you with all joy and peace as you trust in him, so that you may overflow with hope by the power of the Holy Spirit.

Romans 15:13

Our mouths were filled with laughter,
  our tongues with songs of joy.
Then it was said among the nations,
  "The LORD has done great things for them."
The LORD has done great things for us,
  and we are filled with joy.

Psalm 126:2–3

I will rejoice in the LORD,
  I will be joyful in God my Savior.

Habakkuk 3:18

Jesus said, "As the Father has loved me, so have I loved you. Now remain in my love. If you obey my commands, you will remain in my love, just as I have obeyed my Father's commands and remain in his love. I have told you this so that my joy may be in you and that your joy may be complete."

John 15:9–11

You turned my wailing into dancing;
> you removed my sackcloth and clothed
>> me with joy,
that my heart may sing to you and not
> be silent.
> O LORD my God, I will give you thanks
>> forever.

Psalm 30:11–12

Joy

Sing joyfully to the LORD, you righteous;
  it is fitting for the upright to praise him.

Psalm 33:1

When I said, "My foot is slipping,"
  your love, O LORD, supported me.
When anxiety was great within me,
  your consolation brought joy to my soul.

Psalm 94:18–19

*To [God] who is able to keep you from falling and
to present you before his glorious presence
without fault and with great joy—to the only
God our Savior be glory, majesty, power and
authority, through Jesus Christ our Lord, before
all ages, now and forevermore! Amen.*

Jude vv.24–25

Light is shed upon the righteous
  and joy on the upright in heart.

Psalm 97:11

the source of joy

We can experience joy even in the midst of our disappointments and struggles. The joy available to us is not dependent upon our circumstances or temperament. This joy does not come from "having it all together," or from everything going well, accomplishing our goals or from overcoming obstacles. No, this joy is *"of the LORD."*

True joy is inseparable from the Lord, for it originates from him. It's always accessible to us because he's given us his Holy Spirit of joy to dwell within us! The enemy deceives us into believing we cannot experience joy—at least not just yet.

Yet God wants us to know his joy now. Not tomorrow, not when we're free of sin, not when sorrow has passed, not when we've become successful, not when we've lost ten pounds, not when we've paid off our debt, received a promotion or bought a bigger home, but *now*—this day!

Lasting joy resides in God himself. Take time this day to seek the Lord first, and draw upon his joy to find supernatural strength.

Kindness

A kindhearted woman gains respect,
   but ruthless men gain only wealth.
A kind man benefits himself,
   but a cruel man brings trouble on himself.

Proverbs 11:16–17

*The fruit of the Spirit is love, joy, peace, patience,
kindness, goodness, faithfulness, gentleness and
self-control.*

Galatians 5:22–23

*As God's chosen people, holy and dearly loved,
clothe yourselves with compassion, kindness,
humility, gentleness and patience.*

Colossians 3:12

*Make sure that nobody pays back wrong for
wrong, but always try to be kind to each other
and to everyone else.*

1 Thessalonians 5:15

*Carry each other's burdens, and in this way you
will fulfill the law of Christ.*

Galatians 6:2

As servants of God we commend ourselves in every way: in great endurance; in troubles, hardships and distresses; in purity, understanding, patience and kindness; in the Holy Spirit and in sincere love.

2 Corinthians 6:4, 6

If anyone has material possessions and sees his brother in need but has no pity on him, how can the love of God be in him? Dear children, let us not love with words or tongue but with actions and in truth.

1 John 3:17–18

When the kindness and love of God our Savior appeared, he saved us, not because of righteous things we had done, but because of his mercy.

Titus 3:4–5

An anxious heart weighs a man down,
    but a kind word cheers him up.

Proverbs 12:25

Kindness

Jesus said, "In everything, do to others what you would have them do to you, for this sums up the Law and the Prophets."

Matthew 7:12

"With everlasting kindness
    I will have compassion on you,"
    says the LORD your Redeemer.

Isaiah 54:8

He who is kind to the poor lends to the LORD,
    and he will reward him for what he
        has done.

Proverbs 19:17

I will tell of the kindnesses of the LORD,
    the deeds for which he is to be praised,
    according to all the LORD has done for us—
yes, the many good things he has done
    for the house of Israel,
    according to his compassion and many
        kindnesses.

Isaiah 63:7

showing kindness

G od is the author of kindness. It was his kindness that brought us to repentance and to a relationship with him initially. Since he has been so kind to us, shouldn't we show his kindness to others? As Christian women, we can move beyond the world's version of "random acts of kindness" and perform thoughtful words and deeds. This requires forethought and planning on our part.

Take the time to ponder who is suffering from a recent heartbreak. Maybe they could use a listening ear or a shoulder to cry on. Ask yourself who feels discouraged in your circle of friends. Maybe they need to hear an encouraging word. Think about who might feel alone, and pick up the phone to tell them you're there and you care.

You can show God's kindness in infinite and creative ways. Think about who needs compassion today, then act on it.

Listening

Jesus said, "Everyone who listens to the Father and learns from him comes to me."

John 6:45

Anyone who listens to the word but does not do what it says is like a man who looks at his face in a mirror and, after looking at himself, goes away and immediately forgets what he looks like. But the man who looks intently into the perfect law that gives freedom, and continues to do this, not forgetting what he has heard, but doing it—he will be blessed in what he does.

James 1:23–25

Pay attention to my wisdom,
    listen well to my words of insight,
that you may maintain discretion
    and your lips may preserve knowledge.

Proverbs 5:1–2

Whether you turn to the right or to the left, your ears will hear a voice behind you, saying, "This is the way; walk in it."

Isaiah 30:21

Jesus said, "The man who enters by the gate is the shepherd of his sheep. The watchman opens the gate for him, and the sheep listen to his voice. He calls his own sheep by name and leads them out. When he has brought out all his own, he goes on ahead of them, and his sheep follow him because they know his voice."

John 10:2–4

He who listens to a life-giving rebuke
   will be at home among the wise.

Proverbs 15:31

The Holy Spirit says,
"Today, if you hear [God's] voice,
   do not harden your hearts."

Hebrews 3:7–8

The LORD said, "Now my eyes will be open and my ears attentive to the prayers offered in this place."

2 Chronicles 7:12, 15

133

Listening

Wisdom calls,
"Whoever listens to me will live in safety
    and be at ease, without fear of harm."

Proverbs 1:20, 33

We are from God, and whoever knows God listens to us; but whoever is not from God does not listen to us. This is how we recognize the Spirit of truth and the spirit of falsehood.

1 John 4:6

"Listen, listen to me, and eat what is good,
    and your soul will delight in the richest
        of fare.
Give ear and come to me;
    hear me, that your soul may live,"
        declares the LORD.

Isaiah 55:2–3

The eyes of the LORD are on the righteous
    and his ears are attentive to their cry.

Psalm 34:15

listening for God

When was the last time you heard from God? Maybe you haven't heard from him because your ears have been deafened by the silence of loneliness, discouragement or exhaustion. Maybe God's voice has been drowned out by the hum of too much noise from work, family, church and friends. Perhaps you feel too childish—immature, clueless—to encounter God.

God cherishes our focused attention and waits for us to learn his voice. Then he waits for our invitation to speak into our lives. Be sure to spend time in the presence of God, ears open. Maybe you feel lonely and discouraged. Maybe the noise of the world drowns out God's still, small voice. But if you take the time to be still and listen, really listen, in the silence, you'll hear Yahweh speak your name. Your response can be a simple and childlike invitation, "Speak, for your servant is listening."

Love

Jesus said, "Love one another. As I have loved you, so you must love one another. By this all men will know that you are my disciples, if you love one another."

John 13:34–35

Be imitators of God ... as dearly loved children and live a life of love, just as Christ loved us and gave himself up for us.

Ephesians 5:1–2

This is how we know that we love the children of God: by loving God and carrying out his commands.

1 John 5:2

A friend loves at all times.

Proverbs 17:17

Keep on loving each other as brothers.

Hebrews 13:1

Jesus said, "Greater love has no one than this, that he lay down his life for his friends."

John 15:13

I pray that you, being rooted and established in love, may have power, together with all the saints, to grasp how wide and long and high and deep is the love of Christ, and to know this love that surpasses knowledge—that you may be filled to the measure of all the fullness of God.

Ephesians 3:17–19

May the Lord make your love increase and overflow for each other and for everyone else, just as ours does for you.

1 Thessalonians 3:12

We know and rely on the love God has for us. God is love. Whoever lives in love lives in God, and God in him. In this way, love is made complete among us so that we will have confidence on the day of judgment, because in this world we are like him.

1 John 4:16–17

Love

We love because [God] first loved us.

1 John 4:19

Love and faithfulness meet together;
   righteousness and peace kiss each other.

Psalm 85:10

*Therefore, as God's chosen people, holy and
dearly loved, clothe yourselves with compassion,
kindness, humility, gentleness and patience. And
over all these virtues put on love, which binds
them all together in perfect unity.*

Colossians 3:12, 14

*God did not give us a spirit of timidity, but a spirit
of power, of love and of self-discipline.*

2 Timothy 1:7

*Love the LORD your God with all your heart and
with all your soul and with all your strength.*

Deuteronomy 6:5

Serve one another in love.

Galatians 5:13

Love is patient, love is kind. It does not envy, it does not boast, it is not proud. It is not rude, it is not self-seeking, it is not easily angered, it keeps no record of wrongs. Love does not delight in evil but rejoices with the truth. It always protects, always trusts, always hopes, always perseveres. And now these three remain: faith, hope and love. But the greatest of these is love.

1 Corinthians 13:4–7, 13

He who covers over an offense promotes love.

Proverbs 17:9

Love must be sincere. Hate what is evil; cling to what is good. Be devoted to one another in brotherly love.

Romans 12:9–10

He who pursues righteousness and love finds life, prosperity and honor.

Proverbs 21:21

Love

The commandments, "Do not commit adultery,"
"Do not murder," "Do not steal," "Do not
covet," and whatever other commandment there
may be, are summed up in this one rule: "Love
your neighbor as yourself." Love does no harm
to its neighbor. Therefore love is the fulfillment of
the law.

Romans 13:9–10

Above all, love each other deeply, because love
covers over a multitude of sins.

1 Peter 4:8

the strongest love

God is love—even our desire for love points to him. The love between a man and a woman is a beautiful reflection of God's love, but we only desire love because God places that desire in us and wants us to find our desire fulfilled in him.

The Song of Songs presents a picture of love between a man and a woman that reflects the love of God for the church. God doesn't love you at a distance or remember you as an afterthought. Look at the words used to express his love: seal, strong, unyielding, burning, unquenchable (Song of Songs 8:6–7). He wants you to believe it! He doesn't put conditions on his love. He only asks that you respond to his love: Imagine God saying to you, "I love you so much that I want to be with you intimately, at all times." God loves you with the strongest love imaginable—a love that is as strong as death.

Money

How much better to get wisdom than gold,
   to choose understanding rather than silver!

Proverbs 16:16

Humility and the fear of the LORD
   bring wealth and honor and life.

Proverbs 22:4

*Keep your lives free from the love of money and
be content with what you have.*

Hebrews 13:5

When God gives any man wealth and
possessions, and enables him to enjoy
them, to accept his lot and be happy in his
work—this is a gift of God.

Ecclesiastes 5:19

Do not wear yourself out to get rich;
   have the wisdom to show restraint.

Proverbs 23:4

Lazy hands make a man poor,
   but diligent hands bring wealth.

Proverbs 10:4

otherhood

...amed his wife Eve, because she
...ecome the mother of all the living.

Genesis 3:20

... is exalted over all the nations,
...ory above the heavens.
...s the barren woman in her home
...appy mother of children.
...e LORD.

Psalm 113:4, 9

...t is not proud, O LORD,
...es are not haughty;
...concern myself with great matters
...ngs too wonderful for me.
...e stilled and quieted my soul;
...weaned child with its mother,
...weaned child is my soul within me.
...put your hope in the LORD
...ow and forevermore.

Psalm 131

...hild in the way he should go,
...hen he is old he will not turn from it.

Proverbs 22:6

*Command those who are rich
in this present world not to
be arrogant nor to put their
hope in wealth, which is so
uncertain, but to put their
hope in God, who richly
provides us with everything
for our enjoyment. Command
them to do good, to be rich in good deeds, and to be
generous and willing to share.*

1 Timothy 6:17–18

If I have put my trust in gold
or said to pure gold, "You are my security,"
if I have rejoiced over my great wealth,
the fortune my hands had gained,
then these also would be sins to be judged,
for I would have been unfaithful to God
on high.

Job 31:24–25, 28

The righteous give generously.

Psalm 37:21

Money

Honor the LORD with your wealth,
   with the firstfruits of all your crops;
then your barns will be filled to overflowing,
   and your vats will brim over with
      new wine.

Proverbs 3:9–10

Wealth and honor come from you, [O LORD;]
   you are the ruler of all things.
In your hands are strength and power
   to exalt and give strength to all.

1 Chronicles 29:12

Jesus said, "Do not store up for yourselves treasures on earth, where moth and rust destroy, and where thieves break in and steal. But store up for yourselves treasures in heaven, where moth and rust do not destroy, and where thieves do not break in and steal. For where your treasure is, there your heart will be also."

Matthew 6:19–21

pro

investment

God's definition of
anything to do wi
God's inheritance do
dividends, stock trad
accumulation. Rathe
heart. Humility. Fear
awesome holiness.

In God's eyes, sp
only by rightly relatin
wealth is laced with i
honor and polished f
result in prudence, h
generosity, purity and

You can make he
day that will yield wo
honor and life. Choos
God and serve him w
While these riches of
much in the world's e
count in God's. Take
discern whether you
treasures or those of
investments of the he

Adam n
would b

The LORD
   his gl
He settle
   as a h
Praise th

My hear
   my e
I do not
   or thi
But I ha
   like a
   like a
O Israel,
   both

Train a
   and

144

146

As a mother comforts
    her child,
  so will I comfort you.

Isaiah 66:13

Honor your father and your
mother, so that you may
live long in the land the
LORD your God is giving you.

Exodus 20:12

Listen to your father, who gave you life,
    and do not despise your mother when
        she is old.
Buy the truth and do not sell it;
    get wisdom, discipline and understanding.
The father of a righteous man has great joy;
    he who has a wise son delights in him.
May your father and mother be glad;
    may she who gave you birth rejoice!

Proverbs 23:22–25

Motherhood

May the LORD make you increase,
   both you and your children.
May you be blessed by the LORD,
   the Maker of heaven and earth.

Psalm 115:14–15

A wife of noble character who can find?
   She is worth far more than rubies.
She is clothed with strength and dignity;
   she can laugh at the days to come.
She speaks with wisdom,
   and faithful instruction is on her tongue.
She watches over the affairs of her household
   and does not eat the bread of idleness.
Her children arise and call her blessed;
   her husband also, and he praises her:
"Many women do noble things,
   but you surpass them all."
Charm is deceptive, and beauty is fleeting;
   but a woman who fears the LORD is to
      be praised.

Proverbs 31:10, 25–30

spiritual motherhood

What would you call a woman who sits under a palm tree, mediates disputes, offers godly counsel and takes up weapons to go to war against a fierce enemy? A madwoman? A multi-tasker? How about a mother? Deborah filled each of these roles. She was a prophetess, ruler, mediator and warrior. A woman this gifted at multitasking could be called many things, but Deborah designated one title for herself: mother. Rather than referring to herself as a judge or prophetess she instead called herself, "I, Deborah ... a mother in Israel." (Judges 5:7).

Women do not have to carry, adopt or raise children in order to qualify as spiritual moms. Instead we only need to display a willingness to use the gifts which God has entrusted to us in order to nurture others and strengthen them in their faith. Deborah was such a woman.

Obedience

"Obey me, and I will be your God and you will be my people. Walk in all the ways I command you, that it may go well with you," says the LORD.

Jeremiah 7:23

In everything that [Hezekiah] undertook in the service of God's temple and in obedience to the law and the commands, he sought his God and worked wholeheartedly. And so he prospered.

2 Chronicles 31:21

This is love: that we walk in obedience to [Christ's] commands. As you have heard from the beginning, his command is that you walk in love.

2 John 6

It is the LORD your God you must follow, and him you must revere. Keep his commands and obey him; serve him and hold fast to him.

Deuteronomy 13:4

Jesus said, "Whoever has my commands and obeys them, he is the one who loves me. He who loves me will be loved by my Father, and I too will love him and show myself to him."

John 14:21

Jesus replied, "Blessed ... are those who hear the word of God and obey it."

Luke 11:28

Now all has been heard;
   here is the conclusion of the matter:
Fear God and keep his commandments,
   for this is the whole duty of man.

Ecclesiastes 12:13

Teach me, O Lord, to follow your decrees;
   then I will keep them to the end.
Give me understanding, and I will keep
      your law
   and obey it with all my heart.

Psalm 119:33–34

Obedience

We must obey God rather than men!

Acts 5:29

We know that we have come to know [Jesus] if we obey his commands. The man who says, "I know him," but does not do what he commands is a liar, and the truth is not in him. But if anyone obeys his word, God's love is truly made complete in him. This is how we know we are in him: Whoever claims to live in him must walk as Jesus did.

1 John 2:3–6

Do not merely listen to the word, and so deceive yourselves. Do what it says.

James 1:22

The world and its desires pass away, but the man who does the will of God lives forever.

1 John 2:17

All the ways of the LORD are loving
and faithful
for those who keep the demands of
his covenant.

Psalm 25:10

obey the guide

You may be facing unbearable pressures in your daily life. Pressures you think will get better if you can just *move.* To the right or to the left. It doesn't matter. But throughout their wanderings in the wilderness God showed the Israelites it *does* matter which direction they moved. It mattered so much that he gave them a visible reminder of his presence to guide them: a cloud by day and a fire by night. When the cloud lifted, they set out; when it stopped, they camped. God's sign in the sky marked their course and set the pace. By looking up, the Israelites discovered that the Lord ordains the stops and the steps of his people; that God saying no is just as important as God saying go.

The cloud and the fire also represented their assignment: Obey. God alone knows the reasons of the journey, the unseen dangers ahead and the ultimate purpose behind. He ordered their lives. And he orders ours, if we will let him. Look up and he'll let you know.

Praise

The LORD is my strength and my song;
  he has become my salvation.
He is my God, and I will praise him,
  my father's God, and I will exalt him.

Exodus 15:2

I will sing to the LORD all my life;
  I will sing praise to my God as long
    as I live.

Psalm 104:33

Jesus said, "Let your light shine before men, that they may see your good deeds and praise your Father in heaven."

Matthew 5:16

Great is the LORD and most worthy of praise;
  his greatness no one can fathom.
One generation will commend your works
    to another,
  they will tell of your mighty acts.
They will celebrate your abundant goodness
  and joyfully sing of your righteousness.

Psalm 145:3–4, 7

Every day [the believers] continued to meet together in the temple courts. They broke bread in their homes and ate together with glad and sincere hearts, praising God and enjoying the favor of all the people. And the Lord added to their number daily those who were being saved.

Acts 2:46–47

Through Jesus, therefore, let us continually offer to God a sacrifice of praise—the fruit of lips that confess his name.

Hebrews 13:15

Sing to the LORD a new song;
   sing to the LORD, all the earth.
Sing to the LORD, praise his name,
   proclaim his salvation day after day.
Declare his glory among the nations,
   his marvelous deeds among all peoples.

Psalm 96:1–3

Praise

Praise the LORD.
Praise God in his sanctuary;
   praise him in his mighty heavens.
Praise him for his acts of power;
   praise him for his surpassing greatness.
Praise him with the sounding of the trumpet,
   praise him with the harp and lyre,
praise him with tambourine and dancing,
   praise him with the strings and flute,
praise him with the clash of cymbals,
   praise him with resounding cymbals.
Let everything that has breath praise the LORD.
Praise the LORD.

Psalm 150

Amen!
Praise and glory
and wisdom and thanks and honor
and power and strength
be to our God for ever and ever.
Amen!

Revelation 7:12

sing his praise

Bird songs are glorious, but only human beings can sing with words of praise. And our God who filled his universe with all sorts of wonderful extras wants our praise because he is worthy. God is so worthy of praise that Jesus said if his followers "keep quiet, the stones will cry out" (Luke 19:40).

In Psalm 92 the psalmist recites several reasons why "it is good to praise the LORD."

For who God is—exalted, the Most High, upright, a Rock.

For what he does—great works and profound thoughts, judges the wicked, defeats enemies, is loving and faithful.

This God deserves the praises of all his creatures: people, birds—and even the stones of the field. Whether our instrument is a flute, a guitar or our own off-key singing voices, God wants our praise. Declaring his love and faithfulness morning and night is good. The ability to praise our Maker in song and words is a gift that only humans have. Use that gift and lift up a chorus of praise today.

Prayer

The Spirit helps us in our weakness. We do not know what we ought to pray for, but the Spirit himself intercedes for us with groans that words cannot express. And he who searches our hearts knows the mind of the Spirit, because the Spirit intercedes for the saints in accordance with God's will.

Romans 8:26–27

Hannah said, "I prayed for this child, and the LORD has granted me what I asked of him."

1 Samuel 1:27

Hear my prayer, O LORD;
let my cry for help come to you.
Do not hide your face from me
when I am in distress.
Turn your ear to me;
when I call, answer me quickly.

Psalm 102:1–2

I sought the LORD, and he answered me;
he delivered me from all my fears.

Psalm 34:4

call to you; come quickly to me.
my voice when I call to you.
prayer be set before you like incense;
e lifting up of my hands be like the
evening sacrifice.

Psalm 141:1–2

e LORD directs his love,
his song is with me—
r to the God of my life.

Psalm 42:8

ffered in faith will make the sick
the Lord will raise him up. If he has
ill be forgiven. Therefore confess your
other and pray for each other so that
healed. The prayer of a righteous man
nd effective.

James 5:15–16

the LORD has set apart the godly
r himself;
will hear when I call to him.

Psalm 4:3

*This is the confidence we have
in approaching God: that if
we ask anything according
to his will, he hears us. And
if we know that he hears
us—whatever we ask—we
know that we have what we
asked of him.*

1 John 5:14–15

*Be clear minded and self-controlled so that you
can pray.*

1 Peter 4:7

I call on you, O God, for you will answer me;
    give ear to me and hear my prayer.

Psalm 17:6

I called on your name, O LORD,
    from the depths of the pit.
You heard my plea: "Do not close your ears
    to my cry for relief."
You came near when I called you,
    and you said, "Do not fear."

Lamentations 3:55–57

Prayer

Jesus said, "When you pray, go into your room, close the door and pray to your Father, who is unseen. Then your Father, who sees what is done in secret, will reward you."

Matthew 6:6

Jesus said, "This, then, is how you should pray:
'Our Father in heaven,
hallowed be your name,
your kingdom come,
your will be done
    on earth as it is in heaven.
Give us today our daily bread.
Forgive us our debts,
    as we also have forgiven our debtors.
And lead us not into temptation,
but deliver us from the evil one.'"

Matthew 6:9–13

Do not be anxious about anything, but in everything, by prayer and petition, with thanksgiving, present your requests to God.

Philippians 4:6

I want men everywh
prayer, without ang

1 T

Be joyful in hope, p
in prayer.

R

Pray in the Spirit
kinds of prayers ai
mind, be alert and
all the saints.

I urge ... that req
and thanksgiving
kings and all tho
live peaceful and
and holiness.

"Call to me and
great and unse
says the Lord.

O Lord, I
    Hear m
May my
    may th

By day the
    at nigh
    a praye

The prayer
person well
sinned, he
sins to each
you may be
is powerful

Know that
        fo
    the Lord

our prayer helper

We've all been there. Our thoughts grow so muddled or our situations have grown so complicated that we don't know how to pray. We know we ought to pray. We feel the need to pray. Yet our minds turn blank. *Lord, I don't even know where to start.* The answer is in Jesus; he can fill in the blanks. He knows what you need before you even utter the words.

Prayer is simply a conversation between you and God. You don't have to bend your knees, although you can. You don't have to bow your head—you can look up to heaven. You can pray as you drive your car, as you wash your dishes or as you take your daily walk. You can make your life a continual conversation with God. As you commune with God, Jesus will intercede for you. He'll cover all the things you need—it's what he lives to do.

Pride

Pride goes before destruction,
   a haughty spirit before a fall.

Proverbs 16:18

When pride comes, then comes disgrace,
   but with humility comes wisdom.

Proverbs 11:2

God opposes the proud
   but gives grace to the humble.

James 4:6

The end of a matter is better than its
                  beginning,
   and patience is better than pride.

Ecclesiastes 7:8

A man's pride brings him low,
   but a man of lowly spirit gains honor.

Proverbs 29:23

*Praise and exalt and glorify the King of heaven,
because everything he does is right and all his
ways are just. And those who walk in pride he is
able to humble.*

Daniel 4:37

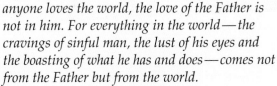

Jesus said, "For everyone who exalts himself will be humbled, and he who humbles himself will be exalted."

Luke 18:14

Do not love the world or anything in the world. If anyone loves the world, the love of the Father is not in him. For everything in the world—the cravings of sinful man, the lust of his eyes and the boasting of what he has and does—comes not from the Father but from the world.

1 John 2:15–16

If anyone thinks he is something when he is nothing, he deceives himself. Each one should test his own actions. Then he can take pride in himself, without comparing himself to somebody else, for each one should carry his own load.

Galatians 6:3–4

Pride

Do not think of yourself more highly than you ought, but rather think of yourself with sober judgment, in accordance with the measure of faith God has given you.

Romans 12:3

I, wisdom, dwell together with prudence;
    I possess knowledge and discretion.
To fear the LORD is to hate evil;
    I hate pride and arrogance,
    evil behavior and perverse speech.
Counsel and sound judgment are mine,
    I have understanding and power.

Proverbs 8:12 – 14

resisting pride

Pride is everywhere in the story of Daniel, except in the heart of the leading character. He humbly credits his survival to God alone. Daniel refused to be sucked into the princes' vortex of pride. Because that's what pride does; it draws others in, destroying everyone in its path.

The prideful princes of Daniel's time may be long gone, but their legacy lives on. Our enemy Satan is called the Prince of Darkness and the Prince of this world. He is a victim of pride himself—his own ego robbed him of his place in heaven. He longs to pull us down to his level and destroy us through our own pride. What better way to fight back than to steal his thunder and his punch line? Because with God on our side, the joke is really on him.

The next time you find yourself gravitating toward a prideful position or perspective, think of Daniel and his love for God.

Priorities

Jesus said, "Do not worry, saying 'What shall we eat?' or 'What shall we drink?' or 'What shall we wear?' For the pagans run after all these things, and your heavenly Father knows that you need them. But seek first his kingdom and his righteousness, and all these things will be given to you as well."

Matthew 6:32–33

Choose for yourselves this day whom you will serve.... But as for me and my household, we will serve the LORD.

Joshua 24:15

We pray ... that you may live a life worthy of the Lord and may please him in every way: bearing fruit in every good work, growing in the knowledge of God.

Colossians 1:10

What does the LORD require of you?
To act justly and to love mercy
and to walk humbly with your God.

Micah 6:8

Jesus said, "Whoever wants to become great among you must be your servant, and whoever wants to be first must be your slave—just as the Son of Man did not come to be served, but to serve, and to give his life as a ransom for many."

Matthew 20:26–28

Jesus said, "If anyone would come after me, he must deny himself and take up his cross daily and follow me. For whoever wants to save his life will lose it, but whoever loses his life for me will save it. What good is it for a man to gain the whole world, and yet lose or forfeit his very self?"

Luke 9:23–25

Priorities

This is what the LORD says:
"Let not the wise man boast of his wisdom
    or the strong man boast of his strength
    or the rich man boast of his riches,
but let him who boasts boast about this:
    that he understands and knows me,
that I am the LORD, who exercises kindness,
    justice and righteousness on earth,
    for in these I delight."

Jeremiah 9:23–24

If I speak in the tongues of men and of angels, but have not love, I am only a resounding gong or a clanging cymbal. If I have the gift of prophecy and can fathom all mysteries and all knowledge, and if I have a faith that can move mountains, but have not love, I am nothing. If I give all I possess to the poor and surrender my body to the flames, but have not love, I gain nothing.

1 Corinthians 13:1–3

the first thing to do

What is the first thing on your "to-do list" each day? What is your number-one priority? Eliminate your kids' hunger? Disarm family disputes? Tackle the budget? Or when you get up, do you put your house in order by putting your heart in order? The best way to run a home, a business or a country is from our knees first thing in the morning.

We can take our cue from Hezekiah, and from David, and from Jesus. Each of these men gave their relationship to God top priority. David wrote, "In the morning, O LORD, ... I lay my requests before you" (Psalm 5:3). And Mark tells us that, "Very early in the morning, ... Jesus ... prayed" (Mark 1:35). They put first things first, and God took first place.

We have only a short time to make a difference to the people in our lives. Let's make worshiping God and leading others to worship our number-one priority.

Relationship with God

I keep asking that the God of our Lord Jesus Christ, the glorious Father, may give you the Spirit of wisdom and revelation, so that you may know him better.

Ephesians 1:17

Yet, O LORD, you are our Father.
  We are the clay, you are the potter;
  we are all the work of your hand.

Isaiah 64:8

You have been my hope, O Sovereign LORD,
  my confidence since my youth.

Psalm 71:5

Come near to God and he will come near to you

James 4:8

So then, just as you received Christ Jesus as Lord, continue to live in him, rooted and built up in him, strengthened in the faith as you were taught, and overflowing with thankfulness.

Colossians 2:6–7

"If my people, who are called by my name, will humble themselves and pray and seek my face and turn from their wicked ways, then will I hear from heaven and will forgive their sin and will heal their land," says the LORD.

2 Chronicles 7:14

Once you were not a people, but now you are the people of God; once you had not received mercy, but now you have received mercy.

1 Peter 2:10

[God] is not far from each one of us.

Acts 17:27

Restore us, O God Almighty;
　　make your face shine upon us,
　　that we may be saved.

Psalm 80:7

173

Relationship with God

Jesus said, "You are my friends if you do what I command. I no longer call you servants, because a servant does not know his master's business. Instead, I have called you friends, for everything that I learned from my Father I have made known to you."

John 15:14–15

My soul finds rest in God alone;
    my salvation comes from him.
He alone is my rock and my salvation;
    he is my fortress, I will not be shaken.

Psalm 62:1–2

come near to God

At times the most effective prayers we can pray are the ones that acknowledge who we are and who God is. Often when we pray, we ask God for things. Indeed, this is part of what God wants us to do! However, as we do when we are in a relationship with another human being, we also need to spend time examining the heart of our spiritual love relationship with God. We need to "define the relationship."

Tell God where you are in your relationship to him right now. Near? Far? Where do you want to be? Finally, what do you want to ask of God based on who he is and who you are? Discover the freedom that comes from acknowledging your weakness and God's strength. You may come to a greater understanding that no matter where you are with God right now, his love and provision are beyond what you can imagine.

Sexuality

God created man in his own image,
  in the image of God he created him;
  male and female he created them.
*God blessed them and said to them, "Be fruitful
and increase in number; fill the earth and subdue
it." God saw all that he had made, and it was
very good.*

Genesis 1:27–28, 31

*Do you not know that your body is a temple of
the Holy Spirit, who is in you, whom you have
received from God? You are not your own; you
were bought at a price. Therefore honor God with
your body.*

1 Corinthians 6:19–20

*Marriage should be honored by all, and the
marriage bed kept pure.*

Hebrews 13:4

*The body is not meant for sexual immorality, but
for the Lord, and the Lord for the body.*

1 Corinthians 6:13

The husband should fulfill his marital duty to his wife, and likewise the wife to her husband. The wife's body does not belong to her alone but also to her husband. In the same way, the husband's body does not belong to him alone but also to his wife. Do not deprive each other except by mutual consent and for a time, so that you may devote yourselves to prayer.

1 Corinthians 7:3 – 5

Don't you know that you yourselves are God's temple and that God's Spirit lives in you? ... God's temple is sacred, and you are that temple.

1 Corinthians 3:16 – 17

But among you there must not be even a hint of sexual immorality, or of any kind of impurity, or of greed, because these are improper for God's holy people.

Ephesians 5:3

Sexuality

How beautiful you are, my darling!
    Oh, how beautiful!
    Your eyes are doves.
How handsome you are, my lover!
    Oh, how charming!
    And our bed is verdant.

Song of Songs 1:15–16

Husbands ought to love their wives as their own bodies. He who loves his wife loves himself. After all, no one ever hated his own body, but he feeds and cares for it, just as Christ does the church—for we are members of his body.

Ephesians 5:28–30

God's delight

Sex does not embarrass God. He deliberately created men and women as sexual beings. Many passages speak unblushingly of sex, reflecting God's approval of the marriage bed and his disappointment when we step outside of his Scriptural boundaries.

The married woman shares her body with her husband just as he shares his body with her. If you are a married woman, your body does not belong to you alone, but to your husband as well. God isn't shy about his approval of sexual love within marriage. He made you for your husband's delight. And he made your husband's body especially for you. In fact, he approves so strongly of the topic that he devoted the Song of Songs to marital love and used it to draw a picture of Christ's love for his bride, the church.

Whether you are single or married, remember that your body is holy. It ultimately belongs to God who created it. Rejoice in the love that reflects God's love for you.

Spiritual Growth

Jesus said, "You are the light of the world. A city on a hill cannot be hidden. Neither do people light a lamp and put it under a bowl. Instead they put it on its stand, and it gives light to everyone in the house. In the same way, let your light shine before men, that they may see your good deeds and praise your Father in heaven."

Matthew 5:14–16

I urge you ... in view of God's mercy, to offer your bodies as living sacrifices, holy and pleasing to God—this is your spiritual act of worship.

Romans 12:1

I am the LORD who brought you up out of Egypt to be your God; therefore be holy, because I am holy.

Leviticus 11:45

May [God] strengthen your hearts so that you will be blameless and holy in the presence of our God and Father when our Lord Jesus comes with all his holy ones.

1 Thessalonians 3:13

The grace of God that brings salvation has appeared to all men. It teaches us to say "No" to ungodliness and worldly passions, and to live self-controlled, upright and godly lives in this present age.

Titus 2:11–12

You were taught, with regard to your former way of life, to put off your old self, ... to be made new in the attitude of your minds; and to put on the new self, created to be like God in true righteousness and holiness.

Ephesians 4:22–24

But just as [the Lord] who called you is holy, so be holy in all you do.

1 Peter 1:15

God did not call us to be impure, but to live a holy life.

1 Thessalonians 4:7

Spiritual Growth

You are a chosen people, a royal priesthood, a holy nation, a people belonging to God, that you may declare the praises of him who called you out of darkness into his wonderful light.

1 Peter 2:9

Everyone should be quick to listen, slow to speak and slow to become angry, for man's anger does not bring about the righteous life that God desires.

James 1:19–20

Our father disciplined us for a little while as they thought best; but God disciplines us for our good, that we may share in his holiness.

Hebrews 12:10

Do nothing out of selfish ambition or vain conceit, but in humility consider others better than yourselves. Each of you should look not only to your own interests, but also to the interests of others.

Philippians 2:3–4

healthy hearts

A s spiritual beings, we need to follow a simple three-fold approach to spiritual heart health. First, we should exercise our hearts by running the race of faith: following the Lord wholeheartedly. Moses warned the young Israelites against turning to idols. To keep our hearts pure, we must stay on track with God.

We must also maintain a good spiritual diet. God's Word is described as both bread and meat. God has made sure we have everything we need for spiritual life and health contained in his holy Word.

And of course, we must keep our hearts pure. Thankfully God has an answer for that. When we confess our sins, he cleanses us from all impurities. But we must also be proactive and keep ourselves from sinning.

These prescriptions for living are key to spiritual health. When you follow God's plan, you really are heart smart.

Stress

Jesus said, "Peace I leave with you; my peace I give you. I do not give to you as the world gives. Do not let your hearts be troubled and do not be afraid."

John 14:27

Refrain from anger and turn from wrath;
    do not fret...
        those who hope in the LORD will inherit
            the land.

Psalm 37:8–9

The LORD is good,
    a refuge in times of trouble.
He cares for those who trust in him.

Nahum 1:7

Trust in the LORD and do good;
    dwell in the land and enjoy safe pasture.
Delight yourself in the LORD
    and he will give you the desires of
        your heart.

Psalm 37:3–4

"My Presence will go with you, and I will give you rest," says the LORD.

Exodus 33:14

Jesus said, "Do not let your hearts be troubled. Trust in God; trust also in me."

John 14:1

Jesus said, "Do not worry about your life, what you will eat or drink; or about your body, what you will wear. Is not life more important than food, and the body more important than clothes? Do not worry about tomorrow, for tomorrow will worry about itself. Each day has enough trouble of its own."

Matthew 6:25, 34

God is just: He will pay back trouble to those who trouble you and give relief to you who are troubled.

2 Thessalonians 1:6–7

Stress

Cast your cares on the LORD
    and he will sustain you;
    he will never let the righteous fall.
Psalm 55:22

Banish anxiety from your heart
    and cast off the troubles of your body.
Ecclesiastes 11:10

Commit to the LORD whatever you do,
    and your plans will succeed.
Proverbs 16:3

Cast all your anxiety on [God] because he cares for you.
1 Peter 5:7

handling stress

Talk about stress. Daniel faced the most impossible and dangerous circumstance with the utmost wisdom and bravery. Not only was he exiled to Babylon (modern-day Baghdad), but now he faced an even more pressing drama (Daniel 2:13). We women face our own everyday dramas and we, too, must be brave and walk with wisdom. You may work as the only female employee in your church leadership; you may care for your aging in-laws who have never thought you good enough for their son; you may be faced with test results that leave you only heinous choices for cancer survival.

How did Daniel handle it when faced with some super-dramatic, high-stress situations? He cultivated a relationship with God and clung to his wisdom and power (Daniel 2:20–23). Daniel invited God into his dramas—will you? You may not feel like you can handle the stress, but God can.

Time with God

Sow for yourselves righteousness,
    reap the fruit of unfailing love,
and break up your unplowed ground;
    for it is time to seek the LORD,
until he comes
    and showers righteousness on you.

Hosea 10:12

In the morning, O LORD, you hear my voice;
    in the morning I lay my requests
        before you
    and wait in expectation.

Psalm 5:3

Seek the LORD while he may be found;
    call on him while he is near.
Let the wicked forsake his way
    and the evil man his thoughts.
Let him turn to the LORD, and he will have
        mercy on him,
    and to our God, for he will freely pardon.

Isaiah 55:6–7

Without faith it is impossible to please God, because anyone who comes to him must believe that he exists and that he rewards those who earnestly seek him.

Hebrews 11:6

Jesus said, "Come with me by yourselves to a quiet place and get some rest."

Mark 6:31

I call to God,
    and the LORD saves me.
Evening, morning and noon
    I cry out in distress,
    and he hears my voice.

Psalm 55:16–17

Jesus said, "Here I am! I stand at the door and knock. If anyone hears my voice and opens the door, I will come in and eat with him, and he with me."

Revelation 3:20

189

Time with God

Now when Daniel learned that the decree had been published, he went home to his upstairs room where the windows opened toward Jerusalem. Three times a day he got down on his knees and prayed, giving thanks to his God, just as he had done before.

Daniel 6:10

As the deer pants for streams of water,
  so my soul pants for you, O God.

Psalm 42:1

O God, you are my God,
  earnestly I seek you;
my soul thirsts for you,
  my body longs for you,
in a dry and weary land
  where there is no water.
On my bed I remember you;
  I think of you through the watches of
    the night.
Because you are my help,
  I sing in the shadow of your wings.

Psalm 63:1, 6–7

*In [Christ Jesus our Lord] and through faith
in him we may approach God with freedom
and confidence.*

Ephesians 3:12

One thing I ask of the Lord,
    this is what I seek:
that I may dwell in the house of the Lord
    all the days of my life,
to gaze upon the beauty of the Lord
    and to seek him in his temple.

Psalm 27:4

*What other nation is so great as to have their
gods near them the way the Lord our God is
near us whenever we pray to him?*

Deuteronomy 4:7

I have set the Lord always before me.
    Because he is at my right hand,
    I will not be shaken.

Psalm 16:8

Time with God

The LORD is with you when you are with him. If you seek him, he will be found by you.

2 Chronicles 15:2

Hear my voice when I call, O LORD;
    be merciful to me and answer me.
My heart says of you, "Seek his face!"
    Your face, LORD, I will seek.

Psalm 27:7–8

I am always with you, [O God;]
    you hold me by my right hand.
You guide me with your counsel,
    and afterward you will take me into glory.
Whom have I in heaven but you?
    And earth has nothing I desire besides you.

Psalm 73:23–25

Look to the LORD and his strength,
    seek his face always.

Psalm 105:4

Jesus said, "Surely I am with you always, to the very end of the age."

Matthew 28:20

fitting God in

The reality is, we don't always "want" God enough to fit him into our busy schedule. We will never get closer to God if we rely on our effort and will alone. Jeremiah reminds us of a life-changing truth: God wants us (Jeremiah 31:33). God wants us to know him. He wants us to live a life free of sin. He wants this so much that he took the initiative to write his laws in our hearts and minds so we would never be without them.

In the midst of your striving, pushing and hurrying, the God of the universe isn't waiting for an opening in your schedule. He has come to you. What does it look like to respond to his desire for intimacy? It might mean simply acknowledging his presence, recognizing the truth already written on your heart. It might mean enjoying the freedom that comes when you cease striving and begin to receive the power of his presence and forgiveness.

Trust

Trust in the Lord with all your heart
> and lean not on your own understanding;
in all your ways acknowledge him,
> and he will make your paths straight.

Proverbs 3:5–6

You will keep in perfect peace
> him whose mind is steadfast,
> because he trusts in you.

Isaiah 26:3

You brought me out of the womb;
> you made me trust in you
> even at my mother's breast.
From birth I was cast upon you;
> from my mother's womb you have been
> my God.

Psalm 22:9–10

It is better to take refuge in the Lord
> than to trust in man.
It is better to take refuge in the Lord
> than to trust in princes.

Psalm 118:8–9

Hezekiah trusted in the LORD, the God of Israel. There was no one like him among all the kings of Judah, either before him or after him. He held fast to the LORD and did not cease to follow him; he kept the commands the LORD had given Moses. And the LORD was with him; he was successful in whatever he undertook.

2 Kings 18:5–7

Some trust in chariots and some in horses,
    but we trust in the name of the LORD
        our God.
They are brought to their knees and fall,
    but we rise up and stand firm.

Psalm 20:7–8

Many are the woes of the wicked,
    but the LORD's unfailing love
    surrounds the man who trusts in him.

Psalm 32:10

Trust

When I am afraid,
  I will trust in you.
In God, whose word I praise,
  in God I trust; I will not be afraid.
  What can mortal man do to me?

Psalm 56:3–4

Surely this is our God;
  we trusted in him, and he saved us.
This is the LORD, we trusted in him;
  let us rejoice and be glad in his salvation.

Isaiah 25:9

Those who know your name will trust in you,
  for you, LORD, have never forsaken those
      who seek you.

Psalm 9:10

But I trust in you, O LORD;
  I say, "You are my God."

Psalm 31:14

To you, O LORD, I lift up my soul;
  in you I trust, O my God.

Psalm 25:1–2

Commit your way to the LORD;
  trust in him and he will do this:
He will make your righteousness shine like
        the dawn,
  the justice of your cause like the
        noonday sun.
        Psalm 37:5–6

Surely God is my salvation;
  I will trust and not be afraid.
The LORD, the LORD, is my strength and
        my song;
  he has become my salvation.
        Isaiah 12:2

Let the morning bring me word of your
        unfailing love,
  for I have put my trust in you.
Show me the way I should go,
  for to you I lift up my soul.
        Psalm 143:8

Fear of man will prove to be a snare,
  but whoever trusts in the LORD is kept safe.
        Proverbs 29:25

Trust

Let him who walks in the dark,
    who has no light,
trust in the name of the Lord
    and rely on his God.

Isaiah 50:10

Trust in the Lord forever,
    for the Lord, the Lord, is the Rock eternal.

Isaiah 26:4

Those who trust in the Lord are like
        Mount Zion,
    which cannot be shaken but endures
        forever.

Psalm 125:1

Blessed is the man who trusts in the Lord,
    whose confidence is in him.
He will be like a tree planted by the water
    that send out its roots by the stream.
It does not fear when heat comes;
    its leaves are always green.
It has no worries in a year of drought
    and never fails to bear fruit.

Jeremiah 17:7–8

trust the cornerstone

Isaiah reminded the children of Israel that they could trust the cornerstone, the coming Messiah, to be strong and secure (Isaiah 28:16). And if we know Jesus personally we too have a precious cornerstone and a sure foundation for our lives. Still, we sometimes lose sight of the peace he offers. Instead of trusting God to answer our prayers and do what's best for us, we worry about the future, fret about life's details and wonder if we'll make it through the week.

Today, take some time to remember what God has done in your life and in the lives of others. Maybe you could start recording answered prayers in a journal. Who knows? Maybe someday your children will read it and agree with Isaiah, "The one who trusts will never be dismayed."

Waiting

Hope that is seen is no hope at all. Who hopes for what he already has? But if we hope for what we do not yet have, we wait for it patiently.

Romans 8:24–25

I wait for you, O Lord;
    you will answer, O Lord my God.

Psalm 38:15

I watch in hope for the Lord,
    I wait for God my Savior;
    my God will hear me.

Micah 7:7

Since ancient times no one has heard,
    no ear has perceived,
no eye has seen any God besides you,
    who acts on behalf of those who wait
        for him.

Isaiah 64:4

In keeping with his promise we are looking forward to a new heaven and a new earth, the home of righteousness.

2 Peter 3:13

Consider it pure joy ...
whenever you face trials of
many kinds, because you
know that the testing of your
faith develops perseverance.
Perseverance must finish
its work so that you may be
mature and complete, not
lacking anything.

James 1:2–4

I wait for the LORD, my soul waits,
   and in his word I put my hope.
My soul waits for the Lord
   more than watchmen wait for the morning.

Psalm 130:5–6

The LORD is good to those whose hope is
            in him,
   to the one who seeks him;
it is good to wait quietly
   for the salvation of the LORD.

Lamentations 3:25–26

Waiting

Wait for the LORD;
  be strong and take heart
  and wait for the LORD.

Psalm 27:14

So do not throw away your confidence; it will be richly rewarded. You need to persevere so that when you have done the will of God, you will receive what he has promised.

Hebrews 10:35–36

Jesus said, "He who stands firm to the end will be saved."

Matthew 24:13

Christ was sacrificed once to take away the sins of many people; and he will appear a second time, not to bear sin, but to bring salvation to those who are waiting for him.

Hebrews 9:28

Keep yourselves in God's love as you wait for the mercy of our Lord Jesus Christ to bring you to eternal life.

Jude v.21

waiting in hope

What are you waiting for?

Waiting is hard when you just know your life will be so much better if your hopes become reality. Waiting is hard ... especially when years pass and there is no sign of your expectations being met. Questions begin to dominate your thoughts: *Why don't I have this now? What have I done wrong? What if it doesn't happen?* Often, the longer you wait, the more desperate you become.

But God has plans for your life. Plans that will make you thrive and not be knocked down by life's setbacks. God's plans are well worth waiting for. You may be tempted to take matters into your own hands, thinking God is just a little bit late. But don't risk God's perfect intentions for you by relying on your own schemes. Waiting for God's perfect timing can save you years of heartbreak. Remember, God is faithful and always keeps his promises—even if you have to wait.

Worship

Since we are receiving a kingdom that cannot be shaken, let us be thankful, and so worship God acceptably with reverence and awe.

Hebrews 12:28

Shout for joy to the LORD, all the earth.
  Worship the LORD with gladness;
  come before him with joyful songs.

Psalm 100:1–2

  Ascribe to the LORD the glory due his name.
Bring an offering and come before him;
  worship the LORD in the splendor of
      his holiness.

1 Chronicles 16:29

Be sure to fear the LORD and serve him faithfully with all your heart; consider what great things he has done for you.

1 Samuel 12:24

Worship the LORD in the splendor of
      his holiness;
  tremble before him, all the earth.

Psalm 96:9

*Jesus said, "A time is coming
and has now come when
the true worshipers will
worship the Father in spirit
and truth, for they are the
kind of worshipers the Father
seeks. God is spirit, and his
worshipers must worship in
spirit and in truth."*

John 4:23–24

*May the God who gives endurance and
encouragement give you a spirit of unity among
yourselves as you follow Christ Jesus, so that with
one heart and mouth you may glorify the God and
Father of our Lord Jesus Christ.*

Romans 15:5–6

Come, let us bow down in worship,
    let us kneel before the LORD our Maker;
for he is our God
    and we are the people of his pasture,
    the flock under his care.

Psalm 95:6–7

Worship

Because your love is better than life,
　　my lips will glorify you, [O God.]
I will praise you as long as I live,
　　and in your name I will lift up my hands.
My soul will be satisfied as with the richest
　　　　of foods;
　　with singing lips my mouth will
　　　　praise you.

Psalm 63:3 – 5

*Jesus said, "'Worship the Lord your God, and
serve him only.'"*

Matthew 4:10

I will praise you, O LORD, with all my heart;
　　I will tell of all your wonders.
I will be glad and rejoice in you;
　　I will sing praise to your name,
　　　　O Most High.

Psalm 9:1 – 2

The LORD is in his holy temple,
　　let all the earth be silent before him.

Habakkuk 2:20

Command those who are rich in this present world not to be arrogant nor to put their hope in wealth, which is so uncertain, but to put their hope in God, who richly provides us with everything for our enjoyment. Command them to do good, to be rich in good deeds, and to be generous and willing to share.

1 Timothy 6:17–18

If I have put my trust in gold
    or said to pure gold, "You are my security,"
if I have rejoiced over my great wealth,
    the fortune my hands had gained,
then these also would be sins to be judged,
    for I would have been unfaithful to God
        on high.

Job 31:24–25, 28

The righteous give generously.

Psalm 37:21

Money

Honor the LORD with your wealth,
  with the firstfruits of all your crops;
then your barns will be filled to overflowing,
  and your vats will brim over with
    new wine.

Proverbs 3:9–10

Wealth and honor come from you, [O LORD;]
  you are the ruler of all things.
In your hands are strength and power
  to exalt and give strength to all.

1 Chronicles 29:12

*Jesus said, "Do not store up for yourselves
treasures on earth, where moth and rust destroy,
and where thieves break in and steal. But store up
for yourselves treasures in heaven, where moth and
rust do not destroy, and where thieves do not break
in and steal. For where your treasure is, there your
heart will be also."*

Matthew 6:19–21

investments of the heart

God's definition of *wealth* doesn't have anything to do with the world's definition. God's inheritance doesn't include quarterly dividends, stock trades or accelerated land accumulation. Rather it involves matters of the heart. Humility. Fear of God—reverence for his awesome holiness.

In God's eyes, spiritual riches are found only by rightly relating to him. True spiritual wealth is laced with integrity, bejeweled by honor and polished for eternity. True riches will result in prudence, humility, honor, discipline, generosity, purity and graciousness.

You can make heart investments every day that will yield wonderful results and bring honor and life. Choose to humbly walk with God and serve him with reverence and awe. While these riches of the heart may not count much in the world's estimation, they certainly count in God's. Take some time today to discern whether you are focusing on worldly treasures or those of the eternal variety, the investments of the heart.

Motherhood

Adam named his wife Eve, because she would become the mother of all the living.

Genesis 3:20

The LORD is exalted over all the nations,
    his glory above the heavens.
He settles the barren woman in her home
    as a happy mother of children.
Praise the LORD.

Psalm 113:4, 9

My heart is not proud, O LORD,
    my eyes are not haughty;
I do not concern myself with great matters
    or things too wonderful for me.
But I have stilled and quieted my soul;
    like a weaned child with its mother,
    like a weaned child is my soul within me.
O Israel, put your hope in the LORD
    both now and forevermore.

Psalm 131

Train a child in the way he should go,
    and when he is old he will not turn from it.

Proverbs 22:6

This is the confidence we have in approaching God: that if we ask anything according to his will, he hears us. And if we know that he hears us — whatever we ask — we know that we have what we asked of him.

1 John 5:14 – 15

Be clear minded and self-controlled so that you can pray.

1 Peter 4:7

I call on you, O God, for you will answer me;
    give ear to me and hear my prayer.

Psalm 17:6

I called on your name, O LORD,
    from the depths of the pit.
You heard my plea: "Do not close your ears
    to my cry for relief."
You came near when I called you,
    and you said, "Do not fear."

Lamentations 3:55 – 57

Prayer

Jesus said, "When you pray, go into your room, close the door and pray to your Father, who is unseen. Then your Father, who sees what is done in secret, will reward you."

Matthew 6:6

Jesus said, "This, then, is how you should pray:
'Our Father in heaven,
hallowed be your name,
your kingdom come,
your will be done
　　on earth as it is in heaven.
Give us today our daily bread.
Forgive us our debts,
　　as we also have forgiven our debtors.
And lead us not into temptation,
but deliver us from the evil one.'"

Matthew 6:9 – 13

Do not be anxious about anything, but in everything, by prayer and petition, with thanksgiving, present your requests to God.

Philippians 4:6

I want men everywhere to lift up holy hands in prayer, without anger or disputing.

1 Timothy 2:8

Be joyful in hope, patient in affliction, faithful in prayer.

Romans 12:12

Pray in the Spirit on all occasions with all kinds of prayers and requests. With this in mind, be alert and always keep on praying for all the saints.

Ephesians 6:18

I urge ... that requests, prayers, intercession and thanksgiving be made for everyone—for kings and all those in authority, that we may live peaceful and quiet lives in all godliness and holiness.

1 Timothy 2:1

"Call to me and I will answer you and tell you great and unsearchable things you do not know," says the LORD.

Jeremiah 33:3

Prayer

O LORD, I call to you; come quickly to me.
　　Hear my voice when I call to you.
May my prayer be set before you like incense;
　　may the lifting up of my hands be like the
　　　　evening sacrifice.

Psalm 141:1–2

By day the LORD directs his love,
　　at night his song is with me—
　　a prayer to the God of my life.

Psalm 42:8

The prayer offered in faith will make the sick
person well; the Lord will raise him up. If he has
sinned, he will be forgiven. Therefore confess your
sins to each other and pray for each other so that
you may be healed. The prayer of a righteous man
is powerful and effective.

James 5:15–16

Know that the LORD has set apart the godly
　　　　for himself;
　　the LORD will hear when I call to him.

Psalm 4:3

encountering God

Worship is like the rains that prepare the earth for God's greatest gift. The story of the youthful Solomon preparing to take the throne is a beautiful reminder. The story of God granting this great gift of wisdom opens with a swell of costly and reverent worship (1 Kings 3). Worship creates a context for us to encounter God; it sets in motion an upward spiral where we pursue God and he gladly responds.

Does your heart cry for softening rain? Have you been in a dark place and long for colorful beauty to replace the hardness that has settled into your scorched soul? God can soften your heart if you approach him through simple acts of worship. God can paint a palette of color in your parched life if you ask him for wisdom. Take time to worship. You'll encounter God.

We want to hear from you. Please send your comments about this book to us in care of zreview@zondervan.com. Thank you.